THIS BOOK WAS DONATED TO THE

North Broad Street
Church of Christ

by Connie & Mark Strange

JULY 2009

IN MEMORY OF

Rawden & Ava Clap

Confessions of a Stand-up Theologian

RANDY HARRIS

Abilene, TX

GOD WORK
Confessions of a Stand-up Theologian

Copyright 2009 by Leafwood Publishers

ISBN 978-0-89112-628-7

Printed in the United States of America

Scripture quotations, unless otherwise noted, are from The Holy Bible, New International Version. Copyright 1984, International Bible Society. Used by permission of Zondervan Publishers.

Cover design by Marc Whitaker
Cover photo by David Morris
Interior text design by Sandy Armstrong

Leafwood Publishers is an imprint of
Abilene Christian University Press.

1648 Campus Court
Abilene, Texas 79601
1-877-816-4455 toll free

For current information about all Leafwood titles, visit our website:
www.leafwoodpublishers.com

09 10 11 12 13 14 / 7 6 5 4 3 2 1

FOR MELBA

CONTENTS

Introduction 9

Chapter One: DOCTRINAL DISAGREEMENTS:
                MUST IT BE WAR? 11

I. Looking for God

Chapter Two: GOD WORKS IN ALL THINGS 27

Chapter Three: THE CARD GAME OF LIFE 37

Chapter Four: WORKING WITH GOD 49

II. Three Theological Explosions

Chapter Five: THE EXPLOSION OF GRACE 65

Chapter Six: THE EXPLOSION OF EXPERIENCE 75

Chapter Seven: THE EXPLOSION OF PRESENCE 87

III. Navigating the Brave New World

Chapter Eight: LIFE AFTER THE DEATH OF HUMANITY 99

Chapter Nine: GOSPEL AFTER THE DEATH OF TRUTH 111

IV. The Kingdoms of Earth and the Kingdom of God

Chapter Ten: GOD'S KINGDOM OVER ALL 125

Chapter Eleven: POWER OR POWERLESSNESS? 139

Chapter Twelve: AMERICA OR CHRISTIANITY? 151

INTRODUCTION

Theology must not be left to the theologians. It should be done in the church and for the church. I've spent much of the last twenty years encouraging serious, gracious discussions of doctrine among ordinary Christians, not just the professionals. These essays represent some of those efforts. There are always certain dangers doing "pop theology," but the greater hazard is leaving doctrinal discussions to the academics.

For those who have followed my work through the years, there is nothing new here. I have just attempted to put into print what I have been saying about the Christian faith at lectureships and churches. My speaking style has been retained in print (for the most part). The stories and humor (such as it is) are intact. I take theology seriously, but I can't take myself too seriously. Oh...and a word about the personal stories; I have tried to change details or conflate different experiences so no one can be identified (or hopefully even identify themselves). Ethics require this.

I admit a certain unease at seeing this book come out. It is not the scholarly tome every academic secretly wants to write, but I offer it in the hope that in all the churches we will have big-hearted, generous, passionate discussions about what it means to be a follower of Jesus Christ. There are certain points at which the reader will disagree with me. Since this work has been done over a period of years, there are even a few places where I disagree with me. But if these disagreements lead to a closer pursuit of the truth, God will be well served.

Leonard Allen and Gary Holloway did enormous work to help me turn my speeches into essays; without them this work would not have gotten done at all. Thanks also to Jerry Rushford, Brenda Ellis, and David Morris for their important contributions.

My favorite quote comes from one of Samuel Beckett's lesser known works, *Worstward Ho*, and it serves as a fine epigram for this book and in fact all my efforts in speaking about God:

Ever tried. Ever failed. No matter. Try again. Fail again. Fail better.

Randy Harris
Abilene, Texas

Chapter One

DOCTRINAL DISAGREEMENT: MUST IT BE WAR?

N ot to be overly cynical, but I do not see any way that we can avoid doctrinal disagreement. We could solve this problem by appointing a pope or a preaching office of the church (I am ready to serve). But in Churches of Christ we have believed individuals and congregations must study Scripture for themselves and act accordingly. At times we reveal a romantic naiveté and think we will all reach the same conclusions on every matter but it is pretty clear that this has not happened, is not happening, and will not happen anytime in the near future.

Unfortunately, we have been perceived as a factious people for whom every disagreement is potentially divisive. Thus, the not-so-amusing story of five persons stranded on a deserted island. One, a Baptist, immediately sets up a Bible School with curriculum for infant through adult, even though he's the only Baptist on the island. The Catholic builds a great cathedral, "Our Lady of the Island," even though he's the only Catholic on the whole island. The Salvation Army person sets up a red bucket and clothing drive even though there aren't any poor on the island. The other two are from the Church of Christ. They immediately divide and create the East Side and West

Side Churches of Christ. If you can laugh you are probably painfully aware of the truth behind the humor.

In this chapter I will not claim, "All you need do is love each other and problems will go away." Nor will I create a final resolution to all our troubles. What I will suggest is that if we can accept certain principles as true we may find an approach that does not perceive doctrinal disagreement as a "take no prisoners" war. I propose that we wrap our minds around some basic concepts to help us create a healthier atmosphere in the midst of doctrinal disagreement. At the end of this chapter you can decide if this is progress or not.

DOCTRINE MATTERS

I begin with the principle that *doctrine matters*. Perhaps you are to my theological left or perhaps you are to my theological right but, for all of us, doctrine matters. I resist the notion that if you have good attitudes and are a loving group of people, then it doesn't matter what you believe. Doctrine is the rudder that steers the ship. Doctrine matters. And the kind of doctrine we accept either makes us spiritually healthy or unhealthy. Surely you have experienced people whose views are so twisted it made them spiritually unhealthy. I know people whose poor theology threatens their faith in God. I have some students whose hyper-Calvinist leanings are unhealthy, who think God has every detail of their life planned out to the point that God has already chosen the person he or she will marry. But, when he finds her and she hasn't gotten the message, there is a problem with this theology. Her reluctance to marry him can only be seen as defiance of God's will.

Another example of bad theology is when dreadful things happen in life and we immediately conclude that God has done it as punishment. AIDS is God's judgment on homosexuality and Katrina is God's punishment on New Orleans. This is bad doctrine. We get healthier or unhealthier as a result of the things we believe. I am of the opinion that people can believe some things that are so twisted it takes them outside the household of faith. Even though we are trying to create peace in the midst of doctrinal conflict, we cannot say that any old view is as good as any other view. Doctrine matters.

Clarify the Questions

The second principle is: *Clarify the questions.* Consider instrumental music, an old issue that has again become current. Often when this topic comes up the people who are in disagreement talk *past* one another rather than *to* one another. Usually three separate and important questions surface, all of which are worthy of discussion. One question, "Is instrumental music a salvation issue?" That is, if one is wrong about the single issue of instrumental music is that person lost? For clarification, allow me to crank it up. I'm asking, if the person in question believes correctly on every other doctrinal issue and serves Jesus Christ in a more radical way than I do, but is wrong on the lone issue of instrumental music, might they as well be a Satanist as far as salvation is concerned? Do we hold that view?

A second question arises if one rejects that instrumental music is a salvation issue. That question is, "Even though it is not a heaven or hell issue is instrumental music a doctrinal issue?"

I assume that not all doctrinal issues are salvation issues. At least I hope not. I can think of doctrinal issues that have *not* been resolved after long scholarly debates, of which I have been a very powerful advocate of both sides at different times and about half the people I know are on one side and the rest are on the other side. Every doctrinal issue is *not a salvation* issue. Important, but not a heaven or hell issue.

A third question arises. If instrumental music is not a salvation issue then decisions about its use must be made missionally and pastorally. The question then is, "Should this particular congregation use instrumental music in certain settings?" That is a completely different question from the first two. There may be a hundred reasons to do so or not.

Now, my guess is you have people in your church who have strong responses to all three questions and thus three completely different positions. There are some who believe it is a salvation issue and that is totally non-negotiable. There are those who think it is a doctrinal issue and thus have strong views but since it is not a salvation issue they will not draw lines of fellowship based on one's stance on this issue. And then there are those who don't think it is a doctrinal issue at all (God does not care either way) so its use is a question of appropriateness to the situation and its goals.

My point is simply that we listen carefully enough to really understand each other. Just understanding each other helps us not disagree unnecessarily. I really don't have a problem with necessary disagreements. I have no problem with you disagreeing with my views. I do have a problem with you disagreeing with what you think are my views. And if we work at it pretty hard I have some confidence we could come to understand each other and be clear about what are the real disagreements.

We are All Interpreters

The third principle is: *Our doctrinal views are a product of our interpretation of Scripture.* Consider this instance. Someone once asked me to have a discussion about 1 Corinthians 14 and charismatic gifts. I said, "Great. I'd love to."

So I started, "The way I interpret this passage . . ." and he cut me off and said, "I'm not interested in your interpretation. I'm only interested in what the Bible says."

I said, "Okay, my bad" and read the passage aloud.

Then I sat there, and he sat there, and I sat there, and he sat there.

And he said, "Well?"

I said, "Well, what?"

He said, "You just read the passage."

I said, "You weren't interested in my interpretation."

He said, "Okay what's your interpretation?" And on we went.

The point here is that we all interpret Scripture. One does not just read the Bible while the other interprets. We all interpret.

Consider another matter a little more threatening: women's role in Sunday's worship. As far as I can tell, the honest brokers on this question are all trying to be faithful to Scripture. Disagreement is not about commitment to Scripture; disagreement revolves around differing interpretations. This is not to say everyone who deals with this issue is perfectly honest with Scripture. There are some dishonest brokers out there. But let us not leap to the conclusion that because someone disagrees with me that this person is dishonestly interpreting Scripture. We both interpret Scripture. Our conversation concerns our disagreements on interpretation. Disagreement with me is not a refusal to take Scripture seriously. We must believe that in our churches we have people who are trying to be honest with Scripture so we can talk about our interpretations. And if we get to the point that you don't think I'm going to threaten or question your commitment to Scripture every time you come up with a quirky interpretation, then we can have some serious and profitable conversations.

PRACTICE HUMILITY

The fourth principle is: *Epistemological humility*. Which is to say, let us be a little bit humble about what we know. In other words, disagreement with me is not necessarily disagreement with God. If we are not humble about what we know, we are unteachable. Only people who are willing to be humble in their knowledge can be taught anything. I enjoy asking the question, "Have you changed your mind on any serious point of biblical interpretation in the last ten years? Twenty years? Thirty years? Since you were eighteen?" I suppose it's possible that people are such prodigies that they get it all right the first time. Most of us aren't like that.

For example, I've changed my mind on Romans 7. Once I was absolutely convinced that Paul was talking about his post Christian experiences. I had a convincing argument. When a person would say, "That can't be Paul's Christian experience," I would respond, "How's perfection going for you?" She'd say, "Oh, not very well," and I'd feel very proud of myself for having proven my point, which of course, didn't prove anything. I just read my experience over onto the text.

As I kept reading Romans 7, I became absolutely convinced I had it wrong. Now, I think Paul is talking about his experience of trying to be righteous under the law, experiencing a transformation of the gracious call of Jesus Christ, empowered in a way he never was when living under the law. I had been wrong. There have been other cases like this, with even more critical doctrinal issues at stake. But if we aren't a little humble about what we currently believe then we are unable to have open conversations and find it extraordinarily difficult to learn anything new.

Hans-Georg Gadamer somewhere said, "Conversation is not me trying to convince you to my point of view or you trying to convince me to yours. It's both of us trying to be convinced by a third thing, which is, the truth." I'm not trying to win you over, and you're not trying to win me over. We're both trying to be won over by the truth which can happen when we take a humble position before God and the truth and which tends to make our conversations go so much better.

If I'm going to have a conversation with a serious intellectual atheist, for instance, I will ask, "Tell me what it will take to change your view." If the atheist's answer is, "Nothing could change my view," I must next ask, "Why are we having this conversation?" However, it is perfectly fair to turn this around and have the atheist ask me the same question. If I can't specify what it would take to change my view, questions arise, "Do I have a humble enough stance toward the truth?" and, "Am I playing a game or involved in a real search for truth?"

I ask students before they try to evangelize friends from other world religions to think about this scenario: Go back to your home town, into your house and proclaim, "Mom, I have some good news. I've met this boy I really want to marry, he's a great guy, and you're going to love him. Bad news is his name is Abdul, he's Islamic, and I've converted." Run that tape over and over in your mind before you ever try to convert a person from the Islamic faith because you're asking them to have that same conversation with their parents, that same disruption in their life. The only honest way to have conversation with a person is to think about what it would be like to change and then be prepared to change. How can we ask people to be more open to the truth than we are? We are prepared to go wherever truth leads when we are open enough to say, "I may have it wrong."

I know we don't think we ever have it wrong. A quick lesson in philosophy: Everyone always thinks they are right about everything. If you think about it you'll see that's true. You think you are right about everything. I think I'm right about everything. If you asked me, "Why do you hold this view?" and I said, "I hold this view because I think it's wrong," you're going to say, "What an idiot." No, I hold all the views I hold because I think they are right. I've found out sometimes in the past that I've been wrong about something, but now I've changed my mind about it and I'm right on everything again. I also realize that I may find out some place down the road that one of the views I hold is wrong, but I don't know what that is because if I did, I would have changed already and again I would be completely right. Everybody thinks they are right about everything. The question is whether we are open and humble enough to say, "It is possible I might have it wrong." Humility is a trait very close to the core of the gospel. Perhaps God would like to hear us say, "I wonder what I'm going to learn out of this." Not, "What am I going to teach," but, "What am I going to learn?"

SOME DOCTRINES ARE MORE CENTRAL

The fifth principle is: *Doctrinal commitments are not a list; they are concentric circles*. If doctrinal commitments are just a list of things that we believe then everything on the list is equally important. Instead, imagine concentric circles with the cross at the middle. Some doctrines are closer to or more distant from the center. Conversations at the center carry a great deal more weight than conversations in one of the outer circles. This image of concentric circles embraces Jesus' view on doctrine. Consider when Jesus was asked to identify the most important commandment. He didn't suggest that all commandments were of equal importance. He speaks instead about the heart of the matter, "Love the Lord your God with all your heart and love your neighbor as yourself." To the Pharisees he claimed that some doctrine "weighed more" than others. Every issue is not of equal importance.

The conversation of greatest benefit, then, is about which doctrines belong at the center. Which are at the edges? We will not entirely agree but we will have more agreement than we might expect. I have come to understand that in some cases the disagreement with people that I have on small issues is only a suggestion that we understand the gospel in fundamentally different ways. What we really disagree about is what's at the center. And that is a crucial conversation to have. What is the gospel? What is the good news? What is right at the center?

For instance, I don't think millennial issues are at the center. I guess I prefer to adopt G. C. Brewer's view, in contrast to Foy E. Wallace (as the story is told), who thought millennialism was very much at the center. Brewer said, "If God wants to come down and reign on the earth for a thousand years, I'll let him. Brother Wallace won't." Brewer did not locate millennialism at the center.

Begin with Prayer

The sixth principle is: *Theology grows out of spirituality.* It is a lot easier to have doctrinal conversations among prayerful people who have taken seriously the call to follow Jesus Christ in every word, thought, and deed. If we first attend to our spiritual lives, our relationship with God, and are bathed in prayer, the conversations go a lot differently. As I grow older more rapidly, I find myself less interested in fencing over doctrinal issues which will not change the people in the conversation. I'm interested in what will lead us into a deeper and fuller relationship with God. What kind of outcomes in our lives will result? I recently co-authored a book on the spiritual disciplines when, near the end of the writing experience, I became painfully aware that I was not living into the reality about which I was writing. I have found that I am much better at explaining what I believe than I am at living it; more persuasive than discipled. I wonder what happens when I win the argument but the person sitting across from me is more a disciple of Jesus than I.

One of the things that we're noticing in our world is that positional authority doesn't carry quite the weight it once did in most of our churches. As an elder, when was the last time you tried, "Because we said so"? You've probably noticed that that doesn't work quite as well as it once worked. When you must ask for authority, you don't have it. If you must ask for influence, you don't have it. And the way we acquire influence is giving our lives to Jesus Christ over and over again.

ENCOURAGE THE RIGHT DISCUSSION

The seventh principle is: *Create an atmosphere that encourages the right kind of discussion.* In a lot of ways I think this is the most important principle. Different kinds of teachers attract different kinds of students. I attract flaky ones. I attract students struggling with their faith. That's intentional; I pray for these students to be assigned my classes. To be honest, I can say I struggle with my faith every day. When students care enough to struggle with their faith, I want to walk with them. The opposite of faith is not doubt. The opposite of faith is complacency. Anybody who cares enough to doubt is very close to the faith. Because I invite these kind of questions, students will often wind up in my office, and we experience some tough discussions. They sometimes involve church but more often spin off into whether they can believe Jesus is the Son of God. I often begin these discussions by quoting my old friend Augustine, "Only he who truly doubts can truly believe." A big old tough guy will just start weeping in my office because, somehow, back home he got the idea you shouldn't express doubt. When people have faith questions but are not allowed to verbalize them, the questions do not go away; they go underground, where you don't want them. You want questions on the table where you can see them and talk about them.

We must create an atmosphere where any question can be asked, where we welcome questions and create an atmosphere of rollicking good humor about them. Some of the most precious time I spend with students is in my living room. Six or eight students crowd in at once and I say, "Okay, the floor is open." A student will say, "I've been wondering about this." And then off we'll go. A lot of laughter, fun, Bible study, and heresy. These are 18 to 22 year olds and they can come to some strange conclusions. Some will claim the Bible says something and I ask, "Where?" Sometimes we come to positions of agreement. Sometimes we don't get it all straightened out, but we draw closer to the heart of God. Without this kind of atmosphere we rob ourselves of opportunities for spiritual growth.

I sometimes ask students in a course on ethics to defend a position they do not hold. Argue it a bit, try it on, how does it feel? The way to understanding comes out of the right atmosphere. Creating this kind of atmosphere in church is largely up to the leadership. The ambience depends on your model, what you encourage in your Bible classes, what you allow God to make happen.

LOOK AT YOUR CONTEXT

The eighth principle is: *Be contextually faithful.* I do not believe that church looks exactly the same in every context. The "One Size Fits All" church is probably in doctrinal error. Missionaries generally understand this. We have missionaries who plant churches more indigenous to the foreign culture to which they go than some of the sending churches they've left. So, we must allow for some contextuality about the way we do doctrine. My hero for contextual faithfulness is Paul, who is not, as far as I can tell, a systematic theologian. He doesn't sit in the library and write theological treatises because he's having a slow day or because he's in prison and doesn't have anything else to do. He writes theology to particular situations, and the situation often makes his theology come out quite differently. Any fair reading of Paul will see that. For instance, contrast Paul's correspondence with the Romans and the Galatians. Paul provides very different looks at the law in these two books. If one understands law only from Paul's letter to Galatia, that understanding is limited because Paul says something very different in Romans. In Galatians Paul is angry with and opposed to legalists. How angry is he? "As long as they practice circumcision, I wish that they'd just keep on cutting." That's pretty angry. In Romans, Paul says the law is "holy, right, and good." Which view of the law is correct? Both. Rome and Galatia are *different contexts.*

In my own theology, like Paul, I want to lean into the wind. That is, whichever way the wind is blowing, I'm going to lean *into* it, not *with* it. If, for example, I'm at a church where for twenty years nothing but grace has been preached, I'll preach discipleship. On the other hand, if I'm with a congregation that has been beaten up for a decade, I want them to hear about salvation by God's grace. I want to be faithful to the context in which I find myself.

LIVE YOUR DOCTRINE

The ninth principle is: *Doctrine must not be separated from our story and our lives.* Ask these questions: What does doctrine *do*? How does doctrine get *worked out*? I am vexed by the fact that we have tended to think about doctrine mostly in terms of what happens when the church is gathered on Sunday. That's where a great deal of our doctrinal fighting is going on. But doctrine engages us in all of life, and it must not be allowed to be disconnected from our story.

The operative passage is Deuteronomy 6. When a little child comes to you and says, "What are the meanings of the statues and stipulations of the Lord?" Tell him, "We were a people in Egypt and God delivered us." So when somebody asks you, "What is the meaning of the statues of the Lord?" tell them the story. In thinking about how doctrinal commitments are connected to our story, consider a doctrine very dear to us: baptism. Baptism by immersion for the remission of sins is one of our better understandings. The only people who haven't thought that baptism was essential have been Evangelicals on American soil. For the previous 1900 years Christians all knew that baptism was absolutely central to faith. They might disagree about when, who, or why, but they all agreed you had to do it. We went wrong with our doctrine of baptism when we disconnected it from our broader story of who we are as people of God. Baptism is so wonderful because you not only hear the gospel, you see and experience the gospel. The death, burial, and resurrection of Jesus Christ is more than nice language, it is a story being played out in front of us. Keep returning to the story. This is particularly important with young people who do not think linearly, but are quite taken by stories. Just because they don't think in the same sequential argumentative way that we do doesn't mean doctrine is out the door. It just means that we must reconnect doctrine to the story. They'll hear it.

LET GOD SORT IT OUT

The tenth principle is: *Recognize the final judgment of God.* Suppose, for example, that I am in an argument with Bertrand Russell (the "atheist of the century" and really smart) about the existence of God. I'm pretty sure he will not be able to convince me that God doesn't exist and I'm pretty sure that I'll not be able to convince him that God exists. Some of the best tried and failed. But I've always thought that as I'm leaving the room, I would say one last word to Lord Russell. What do you think I'd say to him? Would I say, "You're going to hell"? No. Would I say, "I'm right"? No. My parting words to Bertrand Russell would be, "We'll see," because down the road either I'll not wake up and know he was right, or Russell will wake up and know I was right. "We'll see," because finally God sorts it all out, and it is remarkable how much pressure that releases.

In this regard, a passage that has become extraordinarily important to me is Jesus' parable about the wheat and the weeds. This parable haunted me into making this commitment: If I am mistaken about a person I wish to be mistaken in the direction of wheat and not weed. I am scared to death of pulling something up I thought was a weed and finding out it was God's wheat. You share the same belief. I have never met one person who wouldn't say, in the end, the only vote that counts is God's. Everyone believes this. Let's *live* as if we believe that God can sort it out. Once I was assigned this same parable to preach. The Sunday arrived and the person designated to read the parable just before the sermon was one of my students. Five years before that moment anyone would have looked at the young man and said, "He is a weed, bad news, wild kid." But, godly grandparents took him in. Grace of God worked on his life. He's going to be a fine youth minister. I'm sure glad somebody didn't yank him up. Turns out the weed was wheat.

As Christians today are flexing their political power I'm particularly concerned that our judgments are focused on what goes on below the waist. Our dialogue about values is really discussion about sex. Everyone who's read Scripture knows that God's values go far beyond sex. We need to be careful to recognize God's final judgment. God can straighten it out. There are people less doctrinally sound than I am . . . going to heaven. There are people more doctrinally sound than I am . . . going to hell. Helmut Thielicke said, "I don't believe God is a fussy fault finder when it comes to theological ideas. If it turns out he is, we are all going to hell." We will be saved despite our sins *and* misunderstandings.

In conclusion, I would like to speak on behalf of the people I primarily serve who are 18 to 22, who love God deeply, are shockingly radical in their willingness to follow Jesus Christ, stunningly ignorant, and woefully undisciplined. Am I describing anyone you know? There is a great temptation to lose patience. So, before I walk off to class I try to spend the last ten minutes praying for these students who could turn out to be just about anything. They scare me sometimes. We got into a discussion one day about the ending to Mark's gospel, about which there is great debate. One person said, "I know that the ending of Mark, all of chapter 16, is part of the Bible." I said, "How do you know?" She said, "Because of the way I feel when I read it." She may be right in her conclusions but we have better reasons than "how it makes me feel." These young people can turn out to be anything.

That's why I'm writing to you. Take these young people who love Jesus and lead them on a frolicking, big-hearted, deep examination of the faith. When we lead them deeper into the faith, they will wind up taking the gospel to places that you and I could never go. But if we don't listen to what they say, they could turn out to be anything. Some have experienced awful models.

In your congregation you can create an atmosphere where a doctrinal discussion doesn't demand a fight, but an honest exploration of the gospel. Do some theology. Don't leave theology to the academics; bring it into the churches, on the pews, by the people. Let's get used to talking about the faith in big-hearted, compassionate, and gracious ways.

I thought about beginning this chapter with this cheerless prediction: In Churches of Christ I think that we have before us at least 25 years of sheer misery. As I conclude, I have not changed my mind. I wish we could be spared. But that doesn't mean that it has to be misery in your congregation because the way it's going to be in your congregation is largely up to you. You can have these discussions without going to war. There may be times when people have to go their separate ways. Even then, do it with grace and compassion.

I don't know if you've noticed, but Christianity is in decline in North America. In a world growing increasingly hostile, surely we're not going to spend our time fighting with each other. As we set out on God's dangerous

mission in the world, our theology can get better because we have a generation coming up behind us who have unlimited potential. We can do this. It
doesn't have to be war.

Now, may God place within us a deep longing to draw closer to the truth
as expressed in Jesus Christ and conform us more to his image, so that we
may say, "For us, to live is Christ." May God make us into a discerning, gracious, and compassionate people who love what God loves. May God be with
us during times of doctrinal disagreements, leading us into paths of truth
though the Holy Spirit.

Section I

Looking for God

Chapter Two

GOD WORKS IN ALL THINGS

I am going to talk about what God is doing in the world, what our expectations can be, and what human responsibility is like. Basic issues like that. And for better or worse I'm going to do theology. You know what a theologian is? A philosopher is a blind man in a dark alley looking for a black cat that isn't there. A theologian is a blind man in a dark alley looking for a black cat that isn't there who thinks he's found it. That's what we're going to do here. I'm going to try to help us come to some sane notions about what God might be doing in the world.

I have certain rules by which I live my life. I've developed a list of probably a hundred now. Some of them are more important than others. Never play chess with someone from a former communist country. Andrea the Romanian taught me that one. He used to play chess with me. He would slaughter me, set the board back up where I was hopelessly hemmed in and had no escape. He would turn the board around and play my position, beat me again. I learned a new one recently. Never move a really large houseplant in a room with a ceiling fan. But this one is right at the top of the list: Don't tell God what to do. It annoys him. And I want to be really careful here that I don't hem God in and tell him what he can and cannot do, because it annoys him. In the fullness of time, God will be who God will be.

I'm going to talk about some things that are precious to our faith, and I want to do it gently and with good humor. I want to challenge you to think about what it is that God might be doing in our world. My text is Romans 8.

I consider that our present sufferings are not worth comparing with the glory that will be revealed in us. The creation waits in eager expectation for the sons of God to be revealed. For the creation was subjected to frustration, not by it's own choice, but by the will of the one who subjected it, in hope that the creation itself will be liberated from it's bondage to decay and brought into the glorious freedom of the children of God.

We know that the whole creation has been groaning as in the pains of childbirth right up to the present time. Not only so, but we ourselves, who have the firstfruits of the Spirit, groan inwardly as we wait eagerly for our adoption as sons, the redemption of our bodies. For in this hope we were saved. But hope that is seen is no hope at all. Who hopes for what he already has? But if we hope for what we do not yet have, we wait for it patiently.

In the same way, the Spirit helps us in our weakness. We do not know what we ought to pray for, but the Spirit himself intercedes for us with groans that words cannot express. And he who searches our hearts knows the mind of the Spirit, because the Spirit intercedes for the saints in accordance with God's will.

And we know that in all things God works for the good of those who love him, who have been called according to his purpose. For those God foreknew he also predestined to be conformed to the likeness of his Son, that he might be the firstborn among many brothers. And those he predestined, he also called; those he called, he also justified; those he justified, he also glorified. ROMANS 8:18-30

CAN'T WIN

Have you ever been in a situation where it just seemed like you didn't have a chance, you were just destined to lose? One of my classmates at Harding Graduate

School had a brief fling with professional football. He has the ultimate description of what it means to be in over your head. He never got to play in a regular season game, but he did get to play in a preseason game against the Pittsburgh Steelers. As an offensive lineman he looks across the line and sees across from him Mean Joe Green. Now for those of you who don't know who that is, we cannot help it if you are not well educated. We will hasten to say he is a Hall of Fame defensive lineman. My friend knows he's in over his head and so he decides to intimidate Mean Joe. As he tells it, "I looked over at him and said, 'I'm going to hit you.' And Mean Joe looked over at me and said, 'Boy, count your teeth.'" My friend said, "I buckled down and they hiked the ball and I hit him and he hit me and he says I went flying straight up in the air; I fell flat on my back; I looked up and realized he had hit me so hard I was blind in one eye." Only then did my friend realize he was just looking through the air hole of his helmet. He knew he had no chance.

You've probably been there at some point in your life. I got into one of those no-win situations here recently. I fly all the time and I don't fly very well, and so I bury myself in a book when I fly. I'm sitting on the airplane and I've got my book and I'm ready to spend the next two or three hours buried in my book. Life is good, but lo and behold a student from ACU sits down beside me. My worst nightmare.

And the student looks over, recognizes me, and says, "You teach at ACU don't you?" And I said, "Yeah, I do."

He says, "Well, I've never flown before and I'm pretty nervous."

I said, "Okay."

He says, "Would you do something to help me pass the time so I don't think about it so much."

"What do you have in mind?"

He said, "Let's tell riddles."

"I can't think of anything I would rather do."

"I'll tell you one and you tell me one and we'll just tell riddles."

I'm thinking, "Oh brother!"

He says, "Would it be okay if we wagered on them, that way it will make it more interesting."

I thought, "Well, that's not a very good idea, but he's a freshman. Perhaps he can learn something from this experience."

"Sure, why not."

"Well now, I'm just a freshman and you're this very experienced, educated, and sophisticated professor."

I couldn't argue with that.

So he says, "I need some sort of handicap here."

And I said, "Well, what do you have in mind?"

"Well, when you stump me, I'll give you five dollars and when I stump you, you give me ten."

I said, "That sounds okay. You can even go first."

"What's red, white and blue, has green polka dots, reads the newspaper, but never learns anything?"

I'm wondering how many of those riddles he has. I said, "I don't know what's red, white and blue, has green polka dots and reads the newspaper every day, so I give up."

I hand him ten dollars.

I said, "What is it?"

He says, "I don't know either," and handed me five.

CAN'T LOSE

I'm trying to be gentle, but you've all been there right? Can't win. Can't win. This is the text that tells you as a Christian you can't lose. And it is an amazing text because it is so honest. You notice the word that keeps recurring: "Groan." The world is groaning in travail and we the children of God are groaning in travail, waiting for what God is going to do. The twin towers fall and the world groans. The Middle East fights and the world groans. You go to the burn unit in the hospital and the world groans in travail. And you go to the counseling center and you go to the divorce courts and the world groans in travail. And we of all people ought to be the ones who take the groaning of the world seriously.

But this text tells us that as the world is groaning in travail it is giving birth to something, that this suffering is meaningful because God is doing something. In fact, in verse 28 is this astounding, often mistranslated verse; it says that in all things God works. We have to be really careful and read that verse correctly. That verse doesn't say God does everything. What it says is that in whatever happens God will crawl inside of it and work. He'll do something with whatever happens in the world. And God is so accomplished at what he does that in the end he will take all of that groaning in travail and bring all things to the point where every knee bows and every tongue confesses that Jesus is Lord. And nothing in all creation can stop God from doing what he intends to do. In all things God works.

That's hard to believe sometimes. I do a lot of mentoring groups with students. I take a new group of students every year and keep them for their careers at ACU, so I always have three or four mentoring groups going at the same time. And I work mostly with Bible majors. So I had a bunch of Bible majors in a mentoring group one day and I said, "I want you to dream for me. I want you to tell me what you see yourself doing ten years from now." I have ten in the room and they go around and, lo and behold, four out of the ten, 40%, say what they want to do is go evangelize a Muslim country. Before the events of 9/11/2001, the Muslim countries weren't even on our radar screen. Nobody cared. I'm not saying the events of that day were good. I don't believe they were, nor am I saying that God did them. I don't believe God did. What I believe is this: God works in all things. And out of the rubble he raises up missionaries.

Another day we were sitting in the room and one of the guys is just weeping. His parents were going through a very difficult divorce. I've seen the pattern that couples often work very hard to hold their marriages together while their children are at home and when they go off to college the parents break up; so it's not too unusual to have freshman students whose parents are going through a divorce. He finds out about the finalization of the divorce by email. He's weeping and trying to work through his feelings and I'm trying to minister to him and doing a miserable job, and finally I look around the room and I realize I have three other guys in the group who have been through that. So finally I shut up and I back up and I say, "David, do you have anything you want to say to this young man?" And I watch them start to minister to him and put him back together in ways that I never could. And I'm not telling you the divorces their parents went through were good things; nor am I telling you that God did it. What I'm saying is this: God works in all things. And out of the rubble God raises up ministers.

One of the things we do as Christians is try to pay attention to what God might be able to do in the world, especially with the broken places in our lives. Those aren't good things. They generally aren't things God does to us. This Romans passage says God can crawl in the middle of it because he works in all things and nothing can stand in the way of God reconciling all things to himself. If we're going to talk about what God is doing in the world, this is where we have to start. We have to believe and live out the reality that God is taking things somewhere and that nothing can stop it. And our task then is to join God in his reconciling work that he began before creation. He knew you and chose you and called you to be part of his reconciling work, this passage says. So we join God in what he's trying to do in the world.

Two guys are sitting in a bar. Drinking. People do that when they go a bar. And they're watching TV. They see a news bulletin showing a guy standing on the ledge of a building. He looks as if he's getting ready to jump and there are policemen and fireman and trucks everywhere. One of the guys in the bar says to the other, "Bet you ten dollars he jumps." And the other guy says, "You're crazy. He's not going to jump off there. I'll take that bet." And about that time the man jumps. The guy gets out his billfold and hands over the ten dollars. The other guy laughs and says, "I can't take your money. That news bulletin was a video. I saw it earlier in the day." The other guy says, "Oh, keep the money. I saw it earlier in the day too. I just didn't think he'd jump again."

Knowing how it comes out really ought to change the way we act a little bit. We ought to live like people who have hope. Paul says people don't hope for what they already have. They wait patiently for it. I mean when you think about that, this is about as close as Paul ever gets to being funny. I can't tell that Paul has much of a sense of humor, but he almost has some here. He says,

"You know, who gets something and then keeps hoping for it." Have you ever noticed that whenever you look for something you always find it the last place you look? Yeah. I mean when you find it, you usually don't keep looking for it. And you don't hope for it once you get it, because you don't have to hope for it anymore. But he says that as we hope, we wait patiently because we know what God has out in front of us and that he is working in all things.

GOD IN CHARGE

In a world that feels like it is under a curse, this is the crucial starting point. We believe that whatever is going on in the world God can work it into his majestic plan and nothing can stop him from doing what he intends to do. This is what we mean when we talk about God's sovereignty. It is his ability to work his plan with whatever he has to work with. Sovereignty doesn't mean that God has to directly cause everything that happens. But it does mean that whatever happens can't throw God off track in what he's doing.

The patriarchal narratives show us some of the best examples of this. Sometimes God gets to work with people who really cooperate with him and sometimes he's got to work despite them, but whether he's working with them or around them, he always gets it done. Have you noticed? Abraham gives him something to work with. He tells Abraham, "Get up and go." And Abraham gets up and goes. And he says, "Sacrifice your son." And Abraham sacrifices his son. God really gets some cooperation from Abraham. And then there's that time when Abraham has been waiting around for the promised child to come and it hasn't come and hasn't come and he hears a bright idea. He says, "Okay, Hagar!" That was not the best move he ever made. I don't know what God did when that idea came up. I'm guessing God shook his head and probably said something like, "Well, there goes peace in the Middle East for the next 5,000 years." But God found a way. God always finds a way.

Or God has to work with Jacob, who is a sorry individual. When God gets to work with Joseph, he's working with a great guy who just presents God with one opportunity after another to do wondrous things; but then he's got Jacob who is a lousy son, a lousy brother, a lousy business partner, a lousy father, a lousy husband, but a good wrestler, and God finds a way. Because in all things God works.

Or there is King David, who is unfaithful to God's covenant in his adultery with Bathsheba. You don't have to read very much between the lines in the text to know that what God wants to do with David is to kill him. He deserves to die. And when the prophet Nathan shows up and says, "You're the man," it means something a little different than we mean. God can't kill David because David is carrying the covenant. He's carrying the promise. So God finds a way. He punishes David by killing his baby. God help us. But he finds a way. He always finds a way. When we help and when we hinder. When we make good decisions and when we make bad, God works in all things. Boy, does that make life easier. In a world that feels as if it's under a curse, we know that God is working.

JUMPING WITH GOD

A couple of summers ago I had the opportunity to do my first bungee jump. Most of the bad things that have happened to me in my life are because of the company I keep, which is 18 to 22 year old boys. We were out doing some church stuff on a trip to Thailand, and they said "Hey, we're driving right past the jungle bungee jump place. You want to bungee jump?" I said, "Sure." I admit I was lying. So we get out there, and a couple of them go first. Now it's my turn. The jump is 50 meters high (that's 150 feet for those of you who are Americans). It didn't look that high from the bottom, but from the top it's like you're looking through wisps of cloud. And wouldn't you know the Thai guy who's helping me is a comedian. He ties the bungee onto my ankles and says, "Does that look right to you?" I said, "What?" and he says, "I can never remember how to do that part."

Then I'm up on the tower and hopping over to the edge, bungee around my ankles. I'm looking down. Breathing really hard. Respiration is quick. Panting is what it is. Heart rate's picked up a little bit. I'm on the verge of not having to jump because I'm simply going to have a heart attack and fall. I'm thinking, "I can't do this." And then I look at those college boys down there and I know I've got to do this or my life will not be worth living. So I start to talk to myself, "Okay, Okay, Okay." I didn't say it was an interesting conversation.

My little Thai friend behind me says, "Head first." I got the bungee on my ankles. I can't just jump off. I've got to dive off here. I say, "Okay." He knows I'm in a little trouble. He says, "I will count to three and you jump." I say, "Count to 30, please." He says, "I cannot count to 30 in English." I say, "I shall wait for you to learn." He says, "To three," and I say, "Okay." He says, "One, two, three," and I dive, and boy it is a rush. You're just free falling and then you're bouncing around looking at the world upside down. It is a great experience. It really is.

I'm never doing it again. I learned something from that experience. You don't bungee jump unless you believe at some fundamental level God's got you. That your bungee is going to hold. Don't be afraid. God's got you. Let's dive. Because in all things, God works. In our good decisions, in our bad. In our successes, in our failures. In our weakness, and in our strength, God works. And nothing can separate us from the love of Jesus Christ our Lord. The cross stands as evidence that in the worst thing you can imagine, God works.

Chapter Three

THE CARD GAME OF LIFE

How many of you have been to a tool shower? My graduate assistant was getting married. His bride-to-be had one wonderful shower after another, so his college buds decided he needed a tool shower. He registered at Home Depot. Well, tool showers work a little differently than regular showers. For one thing, it doesn't take nearly as long to open the gifts. At a regular shower, you have to open each gift individually, take it out, look at it, pass it around the circle while everyone says, "Ooh. Ah." At a tool shower, you open it up, say, "That's a wrench," toss it down, pick up the next one. After about ten minutes, all the gifts have been opened. And I'm wondering, what do a bunch of college guys do at a shower after the gifts have been opened?

The host then said, "Okay, now we're to the entertainment portion of the shower. We're going to go around the circle and everyone is going to describe their most disgusting illness or injury." And with a bunch of college guys this was highly entertaining. But I had very little to offer here. I mean, I'm a college professor. I'm an academic. Unless I fall off my chair at the library there's not much apt to happen to me. The only thing I could think of involves my two Pug dogs. The reason I have Pugs is because I did not do sufficient research. And my first Pug (named Proko, after the composer Sergei Prokofiev), was unusually stubborn even for a Pug, so I sent him to obedience school. He'd been there for a week. I went to get him and the guy says, "He's not ready."

I had to go home. My dog got detention. So I go back a few days later. The trainer says, "Okay, he's great now. He can do everything."

And sure enough, he would heel and he would sit down, but he didn't like to lie down. I'd say, "Down," and he'd just stare at me. That didn't bother me much, but the dog trainer is being paid a great deal of money to remedy this and so it bothered him a lot. He says, "No, you got to tell him like you mean it. You got to call him by name. You got to do the actions. Use your hand to show him what you mean." And so I said, "Proko! Down!" And I got a little excited and I went too far and I jammed my finger into the driveway we were standing on. My finger split. I now have blood running down my wrist and hand. I'm looking at it. The dog trainer is looking at me. He looks at me for like thirty seconds. Not saying a word. And finally, he says, "And I thought the dog was slow." All of which is to say I have been a little slow about some things.

I've been extremely slow about understanding that people learn in different ways. As a beginning teacher, I was a great teacher for good students, but I was a bad student's worst nightmare. So I've spent the last several years of my life trying to understand the different ways that people learn. Since readers learn in different ways, I'm going to talk about the same thing in two very different ways. First, I'm going to tell you a little story. Then I'm going to do the theology. So if you're somebody who really likes theology, you'll get it in the next chapter, and if you're the one who likes a story, you'll get it in this one. And if you're the one who likes both, then bless you.

How is God working in the world? How do human beings cooperate with God? To answer, I'm going to give you a card playing analogy. I'm going to try to explain everything there is to say about the relationship of God's action in the world and human freedom with card playing. And if that doesn't satisfy you, then later I'll do the heavy lifting with the theology.

GOD AS YOUR PARTNER

There's going to be seven points to this analogy, because seven is the perfect number. Now, the first point is this: When you are picking partners in a card game, God is the partner you should pick. Which is to say, God is ultimately in control. We can see this all over Scripture. The point I want to make is that from the beginning the outcome is not in doubt. One of my hobbies is to watch Satan movies. I know, it's a strange hobby, but I really enjoy them. I like to go to movies that depict Satan about to take over the world. And these movies range from very good to just awful. Very good would be the original *The Omen*. Very bad would be *The Omen 13*. One that really worried me was where Arnold Schwarzenegger was trying to save us from the end of the world. I really thought that Satan had a chance to win that time. What these movies all have in common is that Satan is just on the verge of getting control of everything and winning. But that picture is foreign to Scripture. The Bible paints a completely different picture about the battle between God and Satan. Revelation gives the buildup, then the battle. Here's the buildup:

> When the thousand years are over, Satan will be released from his prison and will go out to deceive the nations in the four corners of the earth—Gog and Magog—to gather them for battle. In number they are like the sand on the seashore. They marched across the breadth of the earth and surrounded the camp of God's people, the city he loves. REVELATION 20:7-9

This is scary stuff. When I read that passage, I immediately think of *Lord of the Rings*. I think about that battle where the city is surrounded by all the enemies and the cavalry hasn't shown up yet and it looks like a hopeless situation. That's what I'm thinking. Scary stuff. Now here's the description of the battle: "But fire came down from heaven and devoured them" (Revelation 20:9).

In the end, Satan's all show, no dough. At the end when he does his worst, it's over in an instant. If you read the book of Revelation, that's really what it's about.

Here's the theme of the book of Revelation: God's team wins. Pick a team. Don't be stupid.

You know, I don't regularly bet on sporting events. I'm sure there's a moral issue there, but for me it's financial. When I bet on a game, somebody will kick a meaningless field goal and spoil the spread. You've probably had that experience. Those of you who would admit it. But if you would let me bet on the games after they're over, I'd get a few right. And that's what you're invited to do. You can pick a team already knowing the outcome of the game. God wins.

Every Thursday night I go over to the dorm to play cards from 11:00 p.m. to 1:00 a.m. I like to pick a good partner because I start to nod off around midnight. Student biorhythms and my biorhythms don't quite match. But as Christians we're given the opportunity to pick God for our partner. So that's number one. The outcome of the game is settled before the beginning. God's going to win.

Playing the Cards You're Dealt

Number two. You have to play the cards you're dealt. Now, everybody gets dealt some cards. Some of the cards you like and some of them you don't. For instance, I had the great good fortune to have parents who were committed to the lordship of Jesus Christ. That didn't have to be. I didn't pick my parents. I grew up in the United States. Arkansas mostly. The land of opportunity. I might have chosen to be a little taller. A little quicker. I once had aspirations of being a shortstop for the Cardinals. It appears that's not going to happen. I might have chosen to be a little smarter. You see, we're dealt all sorts of cards we have to play and we don't choose which cards we get to play. We can choose to complain about it, but you still have to play your cards, the ones you're dealt. For the moment, I'm going to leave as an open question whether those cards are dealt face up or face down with regard to God. My own feeling is there's a randomness to it. But however it happens, I'm going to have to play my cards.

Be a Real Player

Number three. I actually play my cards. This is what we call the doctrine of human freedom. I don't think I pretend to play my cards. I think I play them. God gives me cards to play and then I can do with them what I will. I don't think God plays my cards for me. Later, we'll talk about the notion that God plays your cards for you, what we traditionally would call a form of Calvinism. You know, the Calvinist is the person who falls down the steps, gets up, dusts himself off and says, "Man, I'm glad to get that one out of the way." Everything is set, no true choices can be made.

I really believe you're going to make real choices that have real consequences. You're going to play your cards. Now, let me hit you with why I think that is so important. I'm going to talk more later about the relational nature of God. But, if reality is truly relational, then I've got to be able to play my cards. Otherwise, God is just doing the puppeteer thing.

Let me give you a quick comparison between two athletes. In my later life the greatest athlete in the world was Michael Jordan, because he played his game so much better than anybody else did. Well, back in the mid-sixties the person who played his game better than anybody else did was a baseball player, a pitcher. This pitcher was so much better than everybody else, he could make otherwise competent big league batters look like little leaguers. He was close to un-hittable. His team got into the World Series in 1965 and everybody always assumed that this greatest pitcher in the world would pitch the first game of the World Series, but he did not. Because Sandy Koufax is a Jew. And the first day of the World Series that year was on Yom Kippur, the holiest day in Jewish religion. And Koufax, in an act that is almost unimaginable today, refused to pitch on Yom Kippur. I know of no equally courageous act on the part of a Christian athlete in the last 30 years. Compare that with my favorite boxing athlete, Mike Tyson, who apparently before his last fight had not eaten properly and decided to chow down on his opponent's ear.

If I don't play my cards, if God is playing my cards for me, the worst sinner and the noblest saint are all being exactly and equally obedient to God. Are you with me? Because they're all doing what God has destined they must. Koufax and Tyson are equally correct in their decisions. And I doubt that's right. I'm guessing there's a difference in making good decisions and bad decisions. In being obedient to God and disobedient to God. "Disobedient" wouldn't mean anything unless you have the ability to play your own cards. So I've got some cards here and I'm really going to have to play them and I'm going to have to take responsibility for how I play them. I have students who seriously believe God has already chosen the mate they're going to marry. This is particularly exasperating when the guy thinks he's found her and she hates him. I think you're making choices here and other people are making choices.

God Responds to Our Play

Number four. Like any good card player, God is going to respond to the cards you play. Now, if you've played cards at all you understand this concept. My mother never really quite did. My mother was not a very good card player and she really didn't understand that the cards you play should be somewhat related to the cards that others were playing. We would occasionally have to remind her what game we were playing. But God, who is the ultimate card player, is going to play his cards in response to yours. God does some things in response to your plays that he would not do otherwise.

For instance, prayer is one of the cards that you have to play. And I believe that God does some things in response to prayer he would not have done otherwise. If not, prayer is nothing other than psychological manipulation for ourselves. But prayer is one of the cards that we can play, and sometimes in response to that card God does something that he wouldn't have otherwise done. Sometimes I make a really good play and I think God looks at the card I play and says, "Did you see that? Boy, we can use that. Look what we're going to do with that." And I think there are other times when I play a card and God says, "Oh boy, oh boy, oh boy. What are we going to do with that?" I think God can do something good with our bad plays, but I think God is responding to our decisions, both good and bad, and finding a way to incorporate them into the game that he is destined to win. Now, playing bad cards is not going to affect the ultimate outcome at all, because God is a really good card player. But it does make a difference.

How can I explain this? When my family used to travel, my dad's idea of traveling was to get from point A to point B as quickly as possible and to let nothing interfere with that. Traveling with my dad was something like a death march. You only stopped when you needed gas. My dad's gotten a little older now. He's got to stop whether he needs gas or not. Serves him right, I think. On the other hand, some of you have been on a road trip with your buddies, and in those cases, the destination is just part of it. The big thing is the trip. From the Christian point of view, both the destination and the trip are important.

Now the destination is settled. "Every knee will bow and every tongue will confess that Jesus Christ is Lord," according to Philippians 2. But the trip is important. And the decisions that we make have great impact on how we get there. People do make decisions that lead up to new birth. Good decisions. Decisions that God could use. In a world where it seems as if personal responsibility is flying out the window, we've got to emphasize that the plays we make have an impact on the world. God's going to respond to those and he's going to make it work, but our plays matter.

THE OTHER TEAM SHOWS UP

Number five. Opponents are playing in the game and making real moves. God and I—our team—are not the only ones playing cards. The other team is playing cards. Which is to say, not everything that happens in the world is because God did it. I think it's pretty clear in Scripture that there are powers of darkness who are doing things in the world. Evil people and evil beings act in the world contrary to God's plan. They make real moves. I'm one of those people who take the spiritual world fairly seriously. I occasionally will have people ask me about the occult, for instance. That's something I once didn't take very seriously.

When I moved to Abilene and was trying to buy a house, I got my best friend to help me because I have absolutely no ability when it comes to matters of ordinary life. So I needed somebody to help me from committing house suicide, or whatever it is you do when you mess it all up. We saw one house and I really liked it and I was thinking about buying it and my friend said, "No, you shouldn't buy that house."

And I said, "Why not?"

He said, "Because it's evil."

I said, "What?"

And he says, "The woman who lives there, she's a witch."

And I said, "Well, she didn't seem that bad to me."

And he says, "No! She's a witch! Didn't you see the witch stuff all over the house?" I said, "No."

So I told the real estate agent later in the day, I want to go back to that house again. I had already decided I didn't want to buy it, but I wanted to see the witch stuff, because apparently I missed it the first time. And so we go through the house and sure enough there's witch stuff everywhere. There are pentagrams, there are crystals, there are Druid books. I saw the black cat the first time. I just thought it was in bad taste, but it was there. To this day I do not know whether the broom in the kitchen actually counts or not. But come to find out, in Abilene, Texas of all places, which is not exactly the metropolitan center of the universe, we have a very active Wicca community. A very active coven of witches.

Your gut reaction may be to say, "Oh, what silliness." It was the same with the Church of Satan back in my younger years. I read the Satanic Bible, and Anton LaVey was very interesting to me. He was the head of the Church of Satan. Those of you who have a Church of Christ background will appreciate this. There was a time when a Christian college group had a telephone interview with Anton LaVey and they asked him if he believed that only the members of his church were going to hell. I don't think he had the background to appreciate that question, but we do, right? In actuality, the Satanic Bible is largely about giving you an excuse to do whatever it is you want to do.

Then there are Ouija boards. But I've changed a lot in how I respond to all that. You know, what I say these days about Wicca and satanic worship and Ouija boards and the occult generally is this: I don't think you ought to have anything to do with it, not because I think it's silly, but because I think it's dangerous. Because I believe in the spiritual world, and you shouldn't be invoking spirits that you don't want to show up. Just as I can pray to God, I can appeal to other sorts of beings that I think are real and active in the world. And I think there are people who have sold out to the powers of darkness, and boy can they do some dark things in the world. I don't think Jesus Christ conducted the Spanish Inquisition. I think people did. I don't think God knocked down the Twin Towers. I think people did. And there are real evil entities and evil people playing their cards in the world.

You Lose Some Hands

Number six is very important. The powers of darkness win some hands. No one experiences life as an unbroken string of spiritual successes. We all have our spiritual failures. Peter's denial of Jesus. Abraham's lying about his relationship to his wife. David's adultery with Bathsheba and what amounts to the murder of Uriah. Peter's giving in to Jewish legalism when he should have been standing for the freedom of the gospel. And those are the easy ones to talk about because those people are dead. We have it in our own lives too. No one experiences life as an unbroken string of spiritual successes. There are times when the powers of darkness have their day. We have the low point in the book of Revelation where the faithful witnesses are martyred. You remember? Their bodies are desecrated and the whole world celebrates their death. At the darkest point in the book of Revelation, it appears that the powers of darkness have won.

We Win in the End

Which brings me to number seven, which is just like number one. In the fullness of time, God will finish what he started. After the powers of darkness have won what hands they will win, in the end every knee will bow and every tongue will confess that Jesus is Lord. I want to show you my favorite passage in the Bible, 2 Corinthians 1. I like this passage so much because Paul's ministry had never gone worse than it's going at the time he wrote 2 Corinthians. He has just had an absolutely disastrous experience in Asia. He has also made a mess of the Corinthians' situation. People are crawling up Paul's back and accusing him of being incompetent and unreliable.

Look at what he says about the experience in Asia, "We do not want you to be uninformed, brothers, about the hardships we suffered in the province of Asia. We were under great pressure, far beyond our ability to endure, so that we despaired even of life. Indeed, in our hearts we felt the sentence of death" (2 Corinthians 1:8-9). He says it was a disaster. "But this happened that we might not rely on ourselves but on God, who raises the dead. He has delivered us from such a deadly peril, and he will deliver us" (2 Corinthians 1:9-10). In the midst of this dark disaster of Asia, Paul says there is still a lesson to be learned. When it gets as bad as it can, God is still the one who raises the dead.

And then the single greatest thing Paul ever wrote:

> But as surely as God is faithful, our message to you is not "Yes" and "No." For the Son of God, Jesus Christ, who was preached among you by me and Silas and Timothy, was not "Yes" and "No," but in him it has always been "Yes." For no matter how many promises God has made, they are "Yes" in Christ. And so through him the "Amen" is spoken by us to the glory of God.   2 CORINTHIANS 1:18-20

Paul says no matter how bad it looks, God's word in Jesus Christ is always "Yes." And that's why we're the people who say "Amen." "Yes" is a great word. Just ask any kid. You know, I have sometimes thought that on the tombstone of this generation you can write two words. One is a kid word and one is a parent word. The kid word is "Whatever." Boy, there's a frustrating one. If a kid ever hits you with "Whatever" that means, "You're not going to get me involved, I'm not interested." I had a student who, every time I'd try to get him into a serious conversation, would get frustrated and say, "Whatever." Made me so mad. He was the only kid whose test I ever just graded randomly. I just went through and marked stuff. He brings it back and says, "This isn't right." And I said, "Whatever."

The parent word? "Maybe." Yeah, maybe. "Maybe" is what you say when you can't figure it out, right? "Maybe" is the way that you act polite and say nothing. "Maybe" is the way you keep your options open. Have you ever thought about how little content there is in the word "maybe"? Are you going to be there? "Maybe." That means maybe you will and maybe you won't. But in a world of whatevers and maybes, Paul says God's word in Jesus Christ is always "Yes!" Yes is a great word. Kids know how to say it. I had this poor student in my office once. He was trying to graduate. We were rooting for him. It was his sixth year. I mean, we had all his money, so there was no reason for him to stay. He was just a terrible student. I had him in class one time. He had missed class so often that I left a make-up test for him once with several other make-up tests for other classes and he took a make-up test for the wrong class and didn't know it. I said, "Didn't you find that test pretty hard?" He says, "Well. Yeah, but I find all your tests pretty hard." I said, "You took the test for the wrong class." And he says, "Okay, that would explain it." I said, "Would you like to take the test for the right class?" And he says, "I don't know, what did I make on the wrong test?" In this class you only had to make 60 to pass. But he looked like he might not make it, and I'm figuring the grade and it comes out to something like 59.75. He looks at me. I look at him. I think about having him in class again. I said, "I'm going to round that up!" And he said, "Yes!"

In 2 Corinthians 1: 20 that's what kind of a "yes" it is. When God looks at you through Jesus Christ what he says is "Yes" every time. And we say "Amen" to the glory of God.

When you're back at point number six and the powers of darkness are doing their worst, it is really important that you remember number seven. And that is, in Jesus Christ God always says "Yes" and in the fullness of time, we'll see it.

I think when I get to heaven I'm going to have a conversation something like the following with God:

God, I did my best, but it's obvious I'm a failure. I set out to plant a church that would represent the diversity that the Bible shows you love. And the plain fact of the matter is, I never got it done. Never happened.

God, I tried to learn to pray. I went out to the desert and prayed with a bunch of hermits for a while. I came back and did a lot of lecturing on prayer. But the plain fact of the matter is that I never really got where I could pray believing that you heard every word. I tried.

And when it comes to living out the radical call of Jesus in every word, thought and deed, I never even got close. I tried. So is there any place here for a failure like me?

I think God is going to say: "You couldn't be more right. You didn't do enough and you didn't do nearly well enough. But fortunately, my Son did it perfectly. You want to know if there's a place here for you in Jesus Christ, the answer is 'Yes.'"

And you know what I'm going to say?

Amen to the glory of God.

Chapter Four

WORKING WITH GOD

I want to start out with the most puzzling of all Christian doctrines—that God is trinity. God is one and God is three. I want to tell you why I think the doctrine of trinity is important. What the doctrine of trinity tells us is this: God's very nature is to be relational. Before the first human being was ever created, there was already relationship in the universe. God was relating as Father, Son, and Holy Spirit. Relationship is not something that comes along somewhere later down the line. Relationship is the very nature of reality.

My friend Augustine died in 430 (most of my friends have been dead for several hundred years; I've found that makes the friendship much easier). Augustine, he was a pretty tough guy in the clenches. There was somebody once trying to make Augustine look silly, an unbeliever, and he says to Augustine, "What was God doing for all eternity before the first human being was created?" Augustine's response was, "He was preparing hell for people who ask such questions."

We can do a little better than that. Before the first human being was created, God was living in holy and loving relationship. That's God's very nature. And that is the closest that Scripture comes to telling us why God would create beings like us in the first place. God's very nature is to be relational and so he creates beings who can relate to him in very special ways. I don't think creating fulfilled some sort of ego-need in God. I guess he was perfectly happy

49

before we came along. Maybe the best way to think about it is this. You may know a family who's got three children, has adopted four, and the house is crowded but there's a lot of love there, and then another child comes along that needs a home and they take that one in too. It's not because they don't have enough. It's not because they need one more. It's because they have such love they just keep desiring to reach out and bring in. God's very nature is so loving and relational that he wants to create beings that he can engage in a love relationship.

Now that may seem a strange place to start, but it is the most important thing I'm going to say. Everything hinges on believing that basic notion about God, that it is all about relationship. That's why I have the views that I do on divine sovereignty and free will.

CALVIN'S TULIP

You're at least probably vaguely familiar with a doctrine that's generally known as Calvinism. Calvinism started with a Reformation theologian named John Calvin, but Calvinism as it exists today is not exactly what it started out to be. That is, Calvin himself would have only been a moderately good Calvinist. The basic doctrines of Calvinism were laid down at the Synod of Dort, many years after Calvin died. Now the great thing about the Synod of Dort is they boiled Calvinism down to five points so we can remember them, then someone named them after a flower. So most have heard of the five points of Calvinism which are spelled out t-u-l-i-p. Here they are. If you're a Calvinist, here's what you believe:

> T = Total depravity. That is, human beings are so depraved that they do not even have the possibility of believing in God. They can do nothing until God does something to them. Belief is not a choice. It's not something you decide to do. It's something God decides for you. The image of God in you hasn't been marred or defaced; it has been obliterated. You're totally depraved. Now, if that one is true, the next four have to be true.

U = **Unconditional election.** That is, God chooses to save some of you. We don't know exactly which ones. God's election is totally unconditional. It doesn't have anything to do with you. It's totally arbitrary. It's totally blind with reference to anything good or bad about the person. It is unconditional. Now if total depravity is true, unconditional election has to be true. If you can't do anything apart from God, then the only way you can do something is if he elects you. It can't have anything to do with you because you're depraved.

L = **Limited atonement.** If the first two are true, the third one has to be true. This means that Jesus didn't die for everybody; he died only for those whom God had already chosen unconditionally to save. Atonement is limited to the unconditionally elected.

I = **Irresistible grace.** If God has decided to elect you, there is nothing you can do to resist. Now, if I'm going to pick one out that I want to keep, that's the one I want to keep. You know, I like the idea that if God has chosen you, you can't escape. Because I have been known from time to time to try to run from God and it's greatly reassuring to know that I will never be successful. God's grace is irresistible. There's no way you can resist it.

P = **Perseverance of the saints.** More contemporarily put, "Once saved, always saved." Once God has elected you, it is not possible for you to fall from grace. You will persevere.

THE TROUBLE WITH CALVINISM

Now, that is the look of Calvinism these days. My biggest problem with the whole thing is that it appears to me not to be very relational. Relationships are always two-way. Relationships depend on the choice of two, not just one. And if Calvinism is true, there is nothing truly relational here because I cannot act other than as I do. It would be strange to me to talk about a puppet having a relationship with a puppeteer. It's not really what we would think about as a relationship. Suppose a mad scientist was to create a beautiful, engaging humanoid robot to fall deeply and madly in love with me. Okay, first of all, I'm not entirely against this, understand. On the other hand, it's not particularly flattering either. It's not anything that you would really describe as a relationship because the very nature of relationships is that you can start them and you can end them. We do it all the time.

But you're probably wondering, well okay, if that's true then instead of "Once saved always saved," what I have is something much worse. What I have is, "If saved, barely saved." If my salvation depends on me being in a relationship with God, the plain fact of the matter is I'm not very good at relationships. I do a lot of things wrong. The security is that you never have to worry about God's side of the relationship. He's absolutely constant. He never leaves you. He never gives up. He just keeps loving and beckoning. And the only way that you can fall out of a relationship with God is to be absolutely determined about it. You know, you don't just slip out of a relationship. You don't fall out of a relationship because of a mistake. You don't fall out of a relationship because of a misstep. You don't fall out of a relationship because of a sin. Those things don't destroy a relationship with an all-loving God. But you can decide you don't want to be in this relationship. If it's a relationship at all, God has to let you go. He's not going to force you into some sort of relationship that you don't want.

Now I want to give a couple of extremes and then try to land in the middle. One extreme, which tends to be the Calvinist position, is that God has preordained everything that will ever happen and there can be no alteration in what God has decided. That seems very non-relational to me. The other extreme is what we sometimes call "deism." That is, God started up the world and now he's backed away from it and he's not doing anything at all and anything that happens in the world is going to be because of my choice. In between these two is a true notion of relationship where God is actively engaged with us and we are literally working together. God works in all things. And in and through us. He hasn't backed out of the world and is now doing nothing, nor is he controlling every single thing that happens, because what he really wants is relationship. What he wants is for us to engage with him.

I spend a lot of time in airports, and airports are one of the places where people go to lose their religion. Most of the time when I'm in an airport, I don't really want to talk to anybody. I'm just trying to get from one place to another. I seldom read my Bible in the airport because people want to talk to me who I don't want to talk to. If I'm going to read my Bible, I'll put it in the middle of a big philosophy book and no one will talk to me. I'm kind of this grim airport person. But one time I was going someplace to speak on something I had never spoken on before and I was under the gun, so I had to work on my Bible lesson. I'm on the plane working on my Bible lesson. It is one of those flights that is up and down. It's just awful. And the woman sitting beside me has never flown before and she is terrified and green. It was so rough that the airline attendants never got out of their seats. Finally about 20 minutes into the flight this woman is so distraught that she reaches over and grabs my arm. Now for those of you who do not fly, this is a breach of airplane etiquette. No grabbing the person beside you unless you're flying with them. And she looks at me and she says, "How can you work on that?" It's one of the great moments of my life. I don't know where this came from, but I said, "If this plane crashes I'm fine. But if it lands, I have got to have this done."

Now that's basically my decision about life. On the one hand, all sorts of things happen in the world which I do not believe are the direct work of God, but on the other hand, since we are in relationship with God, it's okay. In the meantime, we have work to do here.

You cannot live like a Calvinist. It is not possible. You have to act like you have free will whether you do or not. If you're a Calvinist, you really didn't decide whether to read this book, but it sure seemed like you did, didn't it? And if Calvin is right, then you aren't truly making any decisions at all. It's all preordained from God, every last thing. But you still have to act like you're making decisions. There's no other way you can live. Even if you stand still and say, "Okay, I'm not going to do anything until God moves me," you're making the decision that you're going to stand there until God moves you. You can't avoid it. So even if Calvinism turns out to be right, you're going to have to act like it's not.

GOD RULES

Any place I open up the Bible where God gives instructions one is supposed to obey, that is evidence that one can obey. When Jesus says, "Come, follow me," I'm assuming that's a real invitation. He's not really saying, "Come follow me if you are ordained to follow me and if you're not, don't because you can't." When he says, "Come follow me," what he means is, "Make a decision whether you're going to come follow me or not." Or when he says, "The wise one is the one who hears these things of mine and puts them into practice," I'm assuming it is possible for us to act wisely, that is, to put them into practice. I assume that when he says that, he doesn't mean, "Okay, what I want you to do is to put these into practice if you're preordained to put them into practice, but if you're not, don't because you can't." You would literally have to re-read virtually every verse in the Bible, because God calls us to do things out of our relationship with him, which if Calvinism is true, we can't.

Let's look at perhaps the most difficult passage in Scripture. In Romans 9, 10 and 11 Paul talks about God's relationship with the Jews and in the process says some extremely difficult things about God's sovereignty.

> I speak the truth in Christ—I am not lying, my conscience confirms it in the Holy Spirit—I have great sorrow and unceasing anguish in my heart. For I could wish that I myself were cursed and cut off from Christ for the sake of my brothers, those of my own race, the people of Israel. Theirs is the adoption as sons; theirs the divine glory, the covenants, the receiving of the law, the temple worship and the promises. Theirs are the patriarchs, and from them is traced the human ancestry of Christ, who is God over all, forever praised! Amen.
>
> It is not as though God's word had failed. For not all who are descended from Israel are Israel. Nor because they are his descendants are they all Abraham's children. On the contrary, "It is through Isaac that your offspring will be reckoned." In other words, it is not the natural children who are God's children, but it is the children of the promise who are regarded as Abraham's offspring. For this was

how the promise was stated: "At the appointed time I will return, and Sarah will have a son."

Not only that, but Rebekah's children had one and the same father, our father Isaac. Yet, before the twins were born or had done anything good or bad—in order that God's purpose in election might stand: not by works but by him who calls—she was told, "The older will serve the younger." Just as it is written: "Jacob I loved, but Esau I hated."

What then shall we say? Is God unjust? Not at all! For he says to Moses,

"I will have mercy on whom I have mercy,

and I will have compassion on whom I have compassion."

It does not, therefore, depend on man's desire or effort, but on God's mercy. For the scripture says to Pharaoh: "I raised you up for this very purpose, that I might display my power in you and that my name might be proclaimed in all the earth." Therefore God has mercy on whom he wants to have mercy, and he hardens whom he wants to harden.

One of you will say to me: "Then why does God still blame us? For who resists his will?" But who are you, O man, to talk back to God? "Shall what is formed say to him who formed it, 'Why did you make me like this?'" "Does not the potter have the right to make out of the same lump of clay some pottery for noble purposes and some for common use?

What if God, choosing to show his wrath and make his power known, bore with great patience the objects of his wrath—prepared for destruction? What if he did this to make the riches of his glory known to the objects of his mercy, whom he prepared in advance for glory— even us, whom he also called, not only from the Jews but also from the Gentiles? ROMANS 9:1-24

In Romans 9, Paul asserts that part of the explanation for Israel's rejection is God's sovereign choice. The examples he gives are striking. He gives the example of the twin brothers, saying God made his choice before they were born. Nobody can question the sovereign choice of God. That's like the person who makes clay figures and then the clay figures say, "Why did you make me like this?"

Now if you go into Romans 10, you'll see he then turns around and argues that Israel has been rejected because of her unbelief. It's interesting that Paul can say both things at the same time and he doesn't seem to have a problem with it. What's the explanation? God's sovereign choice. What's the explanation? Israel's unbelief. Which of those is right? Yes. Don't you love it when that happens on a True/False test? True or false? Just put "Yes." It seems to me that is what Paul is doing.

Then in chapter 11, he does one more thing. He says Israel's rejection is not final. The last word on this hasn't been written yet. And so in the space of three chapters he gives three different answers to the rejection of Israel, and they are very difficult to harmonize. On the one side, they are rejected because of God's sovereign choice. On the other side, they're rejected because of their unbelief. Oh, by the way, they're not really rejected at all, because the last word hasn't been written yet.

Now that shows us several things. First of all, Paul is more flexible than we are. If you're interested, the opposite of Calvinism is Arminianism. What I tell my students is you can be consistent and be a Calvinist. You can be consistent and be an Arminian. Or you could be biblical. Which, believe it or not, does not have the consistency of either Calvinism or Arminianism. It turns out, consistency is not God's favorite thing. You got to love him for that, right? From one perspective you can say God is in control of all of this. In the meantime, you have to live like you're making decisions because if the plane lands you have work to do. There's no other way to live. And then on the third hand, (if you're a three-handed person) what you have to do is wait for the future when God will sort it all out and make it all clear anyway. You can live with that, can't you? I think that's the healthiest way to live.

Once I went to Gettysburg to look at the battlefield. I'm not really a Civil War buff, but I thought it might be interesting. I took the tour and it was. If you take the tour, they'll show you how the whole battle developed. If you're a

Civil War buff, you know that on the second day the South came close to winning the battle. If they had cell phones, that Confederate money you're saving would be good today. They came that close. But they didn't know how poorly defended Little Big Top was, so they didn't finish off the job. So that fateful third day came, when the Confederate army charged across and got mowed down, what we now know as Pickett's charge.

When I survey the battlefield, I understand what happened that day, the logic of the battle, better than anybody who was there when it happened. Isn't that interesting? I understand the battles better than the generals who made the decisions that day. On the one hand, God stands up here and looks at it all. He even occasionally gives us a glimpse of the whole thing. He says he has been in charge of this from the beginning and is bringing all things to its conclusion. So on the one hand, if this plane goes down, we're fine. In passages like Romans 9–11 or like Ephesians 1, Paul backs up and gives us this cosmic picture of God from the beginning working out this plan.

On the other hand, the people who were in that battle had to decide that day if they were going to charge or to defend, and those decisions had real consequences. Moment by moment and day by day, you and I make decisions that have real consequences. We can't live any other way. God calls us to follow Jesus and moment by moment and day by day we make decisions about whether we're going to do that or not. So how shall we then live? How do we live in a world where we believe God is ultimately in control and where we believe that we must live out and make decisions in response to God?

PRACTICING THE PRESENCE

The person who has said more to me about this than anybody else is a middle-aged dishwashing monk named Brother Lawrence who wrote a little book called *Practicing the Presence of God*. And what he asks is, "Is it possible to experience God's presence in very everyday mundane ways?"

Look very quickly at 1 Kings 19, one of my favorite passages in the Bible. 1 Kings 19 is the aftermath of the Mt. Carmel contest. Elijah has won but the outcome has probably been somewhat different than Elijah imaged. As you remember, they had the contest on Mt. Carmel, God sent the fire down, it devoured the sacrifice, the people cried that Jehovah was God, and they then took all of the prophets of Baal and killed them. And I don't know if you remember anything about Jezebel, but she's a little testy. So she puts a contract out on Elijah and he's on the run. He decides to run to Mount Horeb which we know better as Mount Sinai. The mountain of God. Because he is sure that's where God is going to be present.

And then if you come down to verse 9, we see what happens as he comes to this place. He has spent the night in a cave.

> And the word of the LORD came to him: "What are you doing here, Elijah?"
>
> He replied, "I have been very zealous for the LORD God Almighty. The Israelites have rejected your covenant, broken down your altars, and put your prophets to death with the sword. I am the only one left, and now they are trying to kill me too."
>
> The LORD said, "Go out and stand on the mountain in the presence of the LORD, for the LORD is about to pass by." Then a great and powerful wind tore the mountains apart and shattered the rocks before the LORD, but the LORD was not in the wind. After the wind there was an earthquake, but the LORD was not in the earthquake. After the earthquake came a fire, but the LORD was not in the fire. And after the fire came a gentle whisper. When Elijah heard it, he pulled his cloak over his face and went out and stood at the mouth of the cave. Then a voice said to him, "What are you doing here, Elijah?"
>
> He replied, "I have been very zealous for the LORD God Almighty. The Israelites have rejected your covenant, broken down your altars, and put your prophets to death with the sword. I am the only one left, and now they are trying to kill me too.—1 KINGS 19:9-14

What would you say Elijah learned from this experience? The passage continues:

The LORD said to him, "Go back the way you came, and go to the Desert of Damascus. When you get there, anoint Hazael king over Aram. Also, anoint Jehu son of Nimshi king over Israel, and anoint Elisha son of Shaphat from Abel Meholah to succeed you as prophet. Jehu will put to death any who escape the sword of Hazael, and Elisha will put to death any who escape the sword of Jehu. Yet I reserve seven thousand in Israel—all whose knees have not bowed down to Baal and all whose mouths have not kissed him." 1 KINGS 19:15-18

Well, that's a weird passage even for the Bible. God shows him all of these spectacular things, but he's not in any of them. And then he tells Elijah to get out of here and go do the work he has given him to do. What he is trying to tell Elijah is that God is present, not just in the spectacular things of Mount Carmel and Mount Sinai. He is present in the everyday grind of life. And Elijah must get out there and get to work.

What can we do for each other here? There are some of you who live on the "already" side of Christianity. You are the ones who seem to live on Mount Carmel and Mount Sinai all the time. And we are in great need of you because we need the reminder that God is in the world working and doing things.

On the other hand, some of you spend much more time in the everyday grind of ministry and it sometimes seems to you (like it did to Elijah) that God has fled the field and is nowhere in sight. And we need you to remind us that the whole world is groaning in travail. I've got to tell you, there have been times in my life when the stories of God's spectacular action in other people's lives has made me so bitterly angry I could hardly speak. Because the God who seemed to be at their beck and call was nowhere on my horizon.

So we need each other. We need to remind each other that God is working in all things, but at the same time, if this plane lands we've got to get this done. We've got to work and we've got to minister when it seems God is present and when he's not, because he's not just present in the spectacle of Carmel, he's also present in the everyday grind of life and ministry. And we have to help each other look for God there.

I am very uneasy with the triumphalism of much evangelical theology today that makes God look like a short order cook that serves up whatever we need whenever we ask for it. It's not my experience and it has not been the experience of most of God's people in the history of the world. Now when God graciously responds in powerful ways, the proper response is "Praise God." But we are not to give people a faith that depends upon God doing exactly what they want him to do whenever they want him to do it. That faith will almost surely crash and burn. Because there are times in life when we can't find God and we cry out like Elijah, "How long?" We have to have a faith that runs so deep that we will believe in God not just in the light but in the darkness. In all things God is working.

Say Yes to God

I am not naturally an optimistic person. I consider optimists to be people who do not understand the situation. I am a hopeful person. That's a completely different thing. Because optimism depends on human beings, and hope depends on God. And I believe that God in his ultimate sovereignty is going to bring this all to glorious conclusion. And I believe that you and I have a part to play in that. That God has called his church to be agents of reconciliation and the way we treat our spouses and the way we raise our children and the way we treat the people we work with and the ways we interact with the world, either contribute to or detract from God's mission in the world.

Those decisions are ours because, being deeply relational, God wanted creatures like us who could say "Yes" to him and being able to say "Yes" implies that you're able to say "No." Otherwise, the yes doesn't mean anything. And so we have to live life as if we are constantly being asked by God to respond with "Yes." And as we said earlier, God is always going to say "Yes" to us. The question is, are we going to say "Yes" back to God? I believe in the sovereignty of God enough to believe that if we don't respond with a yes to God, he will raise up the people who will. He'll get things done. But it is our task to make decisions and live lives that contribute to God's work on earth.

You stop every once in a while and ask yourself, "Okay, what are we doing here?" Way back in one of my early lives I was peddling religion door to door in Minnesota one summer. Not a happy task, by the way. You would think Minnesota would be a nice place to be in the summer, but it's really hot and muggy and it's the land of, I don't know, 10,000 lakes or something and each one has a hundred thousand mosquitoes. There were mosquitoes that were as big as birds and we had had one miserable day.

We were trying to sign up people for Bible correspondence courses. We hadn't really signed up anybody for anything. It was toward the end of the day. The mosquitoes were starting to come out. We were going to one last door. We had been chased by big dogs. I was miserable and in a bad mood. As we walked up to the door a cute little dog follows us up the steps and I'm grateful for that. I'm tired of being chased. And we knock on the door and a woman answers. The cute little dog goes in the house but it wasn't her dog. And wouldn't you know it, she had a dog. And her dog and this dog get in a fight in her entryway. There are few things that are really sure in life but this is one of them. You cannot sign anyone up for a correspondence course while there's a dog fight going on in their entryway.

And so in a rare moment of bravery, I dive in there, grab the invader dog, throw him out, and then survey the damage. The woman is in tears. My partner is in a coma. It was another one of those moments; I don't know whether it was spiritual or purely evil. I said, "Hi, I'm Randy. This is my partner and we're from the Jehovah's Witnesses." I'm not proud of it. I just thought at the time God couldn't want us to have credit for that mess. And as we walked away from the door I'm asking my partner who is slowly coming out of her coma, "What are we doing here?"

What are we doing here? We are trying to live in relationship with a God who created us to live and trust in love. That's our purpose. God created us that way and then he looked at us and he said, "Now, that's good." What we're trying to do is call the world to come and live in a trusting, loving relationship with God because we know that is the very purpose for being. And everything we do is aimed at that one purpose.

And in the fullness of time, God will complete the task that he started. And every knee will bow and every tongue will confess that Jesus is Lord. And those who have responded to God's "Yes" with their own "Yes" will live in happy, perfect relationship for all eternity. That's the sovereignty of God.

SECTION II

Three Theological Explosions

Chapter Five

THE EXPLOSION OF GRACE

This summer I learned something that has just fascinated me. I learned about the Monte Hall paradox. Monte Hall was the host of the TV game show "Let's Make a Deal." The program always had the same format. You would wheel and deal through the whole program and then at the end of the program he would pick the person who had been the big winner of the day and ask them, "Do you want to make one more deal?" Then they would trade in everything they had won for the opportunity to pick one of three curtains that Carol Merrill was pointing to.

And so Carol is pointing to three curtains and behind two of the curtains is something like a goat and behind the third curtain is the sports car you've always wanted. So you pick a curtain. And then Monte Hall would always do the same thing. He would show you one of the curtains you didn't pick and behind that curtain would be the goat. And then he would say, "You want to keep the curtain you picked or you want to switch to the other one?" And you would have to decide.

Now, it is obvious to me, as it is obvious to you, that your chances are 50-50 whether you switch or whether you stay. Right? You don't have to be a mathematical genius to know that. I can see you've got two curtains, you've picked one, you switch, it's 50-50. Nothing to it. Well, this show was so popular that somebody wrote to *Parade Magazine*, which some of you still read on Sunday morning, and the woman who had the highest IQ on record was at that time answering questions in the magazine. Someone asked if there is any math on this. And she says, "Well, of course there is. There's math on everything. You should switch. You should switch every time because if you switch your chances are twice as good at winning as if you keep what you've got." Math teachers all over America wrote in to *Parade Magazine* and said, "Math education is in bad enough shape in this country without you giving boneheaded information like that. It's obviously 50-50." And she says, "No it's not; here's the formula." Okay, I've looked at the formula. I do not understand it. It has lots of numbers in it. But somebody drew me a diagram and lo and behold if she isn't right. Your chances are twice as good if you switch than if you keep what you got. Legend has it that one of the world's great mathematicians on his deathbed said, "I still don't think the Monte Hall paradox is true." And then he died.

Let me take one little pass at explaining to you why she's right. When you picked originally, the chances were twice as good you were wrong as you were right. Right? So when you get the chance to switch, you should switch. Because that improves your chances. That's the only pass I'm going to give to that. Because this is not a mathematics treatise.

I just want to illustrate how resistant we sometimes are to new information which defies what our common sense tells us is true, or what we've always been taught. It's really hard to give up a position that seems right to you and that you've always held. What I want to talk about are points at which my faith came into real crisis. Each one was difficult for me. Each move was as hard for me to believe as to believe the truth about the Monte Hall paradox. I hope as we go along it will give you some sympathy with those who have not necessarily arrived at the same position I have or arrived at the same position that you have.

A Crisis of Theology

Theological crises are sprinkled throughout the Bible. A theological crisis happens when new material comes in that won't fit in the box you currently have constructed. Does that make sense? Okay, you have a certain notion about who God is and how God operates in the world and then some information comes in and somehow you can't quite get it plugged into the box. And if that happens often enough, then what happens is that the box blows up.

A few times Israel went through theological crises. I think the formation of the monarchy is a real crisis in Israel. Up until then their view has been that Israel has only one king—God. Thus, if Israel has an earthly king what that means is they are dethroning God. But Israel also is facing a little problem; the place is falling apart.

You remember the last verses of the book of Judges? Things are falling apart. That's a rough translation of the Hebrew. And there is no king in Israel. And so what they've got to think through is, "Is it possible to have a king in Israel without dethroning God?" Their answer is, "Yes," and the crisis is resolved.

A bigger crisis occurs when they're hauled into exile. How do you worship a God who cannot even protect his own house in his own land? In Psalm 137 when the people in exile are told to sing one of those beautiful songs of Zion they ask, "How can we sing the Lord's song in a foreign land?" How do you believe in a God who can't even protect his own stuff? And so they need a theology that's big enough to take in the enormity of the event of the exile. It's crisis.

And when they return home, it's another crisis. Because not everybody goes back home. The return is not exactly happily ever after. It doesn't match up to the glory of the old way. So you have to decide how we are going to take in this new reality. Do we have a theology big enough to take this in? And of course what develops out of that is powerful remnant theology.

I think the same thing is true in the New Testament. When Christianity starts to move from its Jewish roots to the Greek world there's a bit of a crisis there. You see it reflected in Acts 15 where there's a lively discussion whether Gentiles must become good Jews in order to be Christians. It is a crisis. We need a bigger box to take it in. I think what is true in these biblical stories is also true for us today, both in individual and collective ways. I'd like to focus on three current crises.

Not Always Right?

The first one I've called the explosion of grace. This is the crisis of discovering that you might not be right about everything after all. Now, my story is not going to be exactly the same as all your stories because I grew up in a certain place in a certain church in a certain environment. But I'll just hit you with a few little things and you see how this resonates. Among other things, as I was growing up I was the scourge of the Northwest Arkansas Bible bowl. I mean I was good. I knew more facts then than I do now. Some of you can appreciate this. I'm at that point in my life where I am now forgetting things faster than I'm learning new ones. I mean I knew the names of Lot's sons who were born to him by his daughters. A kinky story. You know. Good old Moab and Ben-Ammi. Good boys. I knew the facts and I was a fact machine.

I was also well indoctrinated in theological positions that I believed made great sense. And I could argue those positions reasonably well. My students now contend that I've gotten to the point where I'm a sophist and that I can take either side of a position and whip them with it. Bum Phillips, a great Texas football coach once said about Don Shula, "He can take his'n and beat your'n and then he can take your'n and beat his'n." Now I may have gotten a little bit that way, but then I could argue those positions and I still believe today many of them were right. But the problem was, I didn't even consider the possibility that any of them could be wrong. I was absolutely certain of all the ground I occupied.

It's burdensome to be right about everything. But it also makes life much easier in some ways. I had the complete set of answers to the complete set of questions. At least the important ones. I suppose there were a few things in the Bible that I didn't have entire clarity about but they weren't very important. The important ones I was clear on.

But something happened to me that has happened to a lot of you. My world got bigger and those certainties got less secure. It became clearer that the positions I occupied were not just a product of my careful study and my incredibly agile mind. They were a product of where I lived and what I was taught—my bias, in a word. I found that not everybody in the world saw things exactly like I did. That gave me a life's work, to convince those foolish people who disagreed with me. What became more difficult is when I kept running into smart people and good people who didn't agree with me. And I would say, "Okay, if you weren't so biased about this you could see the truth." And they resented that.

THE PHILOSOPHY OF DOUBT

Eventually I began to put some intellectual moorings on all of this. I started to study philosophy and I saw that over the last three or four hundred years some strange things have been happening. Basically, we have been sure of less and less. It starts with that annoying Descartes. If you could put out a hit on a guy who was already dead, I'd do it. Talk about ruining our lives. You know, Descartes, he's the "I think therefore I am" guy. His great-great-great granddaughter was flying on an airplane once. The attendant comes by and says, "You want some coffee?" and she says, "I think not." And she disappeared. It's a philosophical joke, what do you expect? Philosophers have no sense of humor.

Descartes started us down the skeptical road. Descartes asked the great question, "How can I know that any of this is real or any of it is true?" "How do I know I'm not dreaming right now?" "How do I know" (and this is one of the great moments in philosophy) "that this spiteful little demon hasn't deceived me about everything?" I used to have a terrible time teaching Descartes. But I don't anymore. I can teach it to my students easily. I only have to ask them one question to get them into Descartes. How do you know you're not living in the Matrix? That's the question. How do you know you're not living in the Matrix? Great question.

And then Descartes starts to try to answer the question. He says, "I'm going to doubt everything I can and I'll quit doubting when I can't doubt anything else. Can I doubt God? Yes. Can I doubt the world? Yes. Can I doubt my senses? Yes. What's the one thing I can't doubt? Well, I can't doubt the fact that I'm doubting, because if I doubt that I'm doubting, then I can't doubt anymore." And that's how you become one of the big names in philosophy. So he said that the one thing he's sure of is that he's doubting.

Well, I don't know about you, but that guy is just annoying. What he should have said is, "I doubt, therefore I am." That's what he really means. He said, "Okay now, I know that if I'm doubting there must be somebody doing the doubting, so now I've got me back." Are you with me? I've got me back because I know somebody has got to be doing the doubting because we have doubting going on here so it must be me that's doing it. And then he starts bringing everything else back in.

But the problem with Descartes is the negative move is better than the positive one. The bad news is it was also true of his successor, David Hume, and it was also true of his successor Immanuel Kant. And it was also true of his successor, the existentialists and it's also true of their successors, the postmodernists. Okay, follow me here. Descartes starts out with a beautiful plantation, tears it down and builds a mansion. Hume comes along, tears down the mansion and builds a house. Kant comes along, tears down the house, and builds a shack. The existentialists come along and tear down the shack and they build a lean-to. The deconstructionists come along and tear down the lean-to and here we are on the parking lot.

Umpiring Reality

I just gave you the whole history of western philosophy in five paragraphs. It's becoming obvious that the things that we held certain aren't so certain. And so we have to ask the question, "What are the things that I can be sure about? Where can I dig my feet in?" Ian Barbour in his great book, *Religion in an Age of Science*, talks about three things. He talks about classical realism, critical realism, and instrumentalism. I'll illustrate these three approaches, with a window and with baseball, because anything really important can be said with baseball. Classical realism is the baseball umpire who says, "I call them the way they are." If you like the window analogy it means I'm looking through clear glass. I can look out there. I can see it. I can describe it. I can get it right. That was the position for 1,500 years.

Then we get to critical realism. Critical realism is the baseball umpire who says, "I call them the way I see them." Look what's happened. He says, "I don't call them the way they are, I call them the way I see them." Now there's a recognition that my perspective has entered in here and I'm not just seeing the world clearly. Now if you're using the glass, this is like looking through tinted or opaque glass. I'm still seeing something of the real world, but it's coming back a little bit skewed because I'm bringing something to it.

If you've ever had a conversation with a member of your family, you have discovered that you have a variety of perspectives in your family and not everybody sees everything just alike. And it is so annoying. You know, it's just hard to imagine why they can't see things as clearly as you do. Especially people in the same household. If you start getting the cosmic view and bring in people from other cultures and other radical ways of thinking, we discover we don't look at the world the same way at all.

The great modern parable on that is the O.J. Simpson case. Now I don't know where you are on that, it doesn't matter, it's old news. But it was a great lesson on how people can see things so differently. Looking at the same facts. Looking at the same evidence. Reading the same reports. But they just don't see it clearly like I do. Okay, we got critical realism. My perspective is now having an impact on the way I see things.

Then there's instrumentalism. This is the umpire who says, "They ain't nothing 'til I call 'em." Now we're in a different world here. If we're talking about the window, now we're not looking through clear glass, we're not looking through opaque glass, we are trying to look through a brick wall. This means that we are basically going to construct our own reality. There's some truth to this. Our language and our thought do construct reality to some degree. I give my students a lot of stupid examples of this. If you name your firstborn son Bubba, he will never become the curator of the Louvre. Language shapes the reality. Many of you are old enough to remember when we had that Pershing missile system in Europe. Do you remember what their nickname was? They were "peacekeepers." Now if I build a missile system I'm going to name it "peacekeeper." You just try to get congressional approval for a missile system called "baby killer." Language shapes reality.

I think it is very difficult to be a Christian and come to the conclusion that we can't know anything about the world. You can't know anything about

God. You can't know anything about reality. If you go all the way there, I think the Christian thing is going to be pretty hard to do. My own experience was getting pushed to end this way. Anybody else have this experience? I was less and less sure about everything. I was beginning to wonder, "Okay now, where am I going to plant my feet? How do I know that what I'm reacting to is God's work in the world and not the inside of my own head?" It's an important question. I mean, haven't you had someone describe some religious experience and your reaction to it was, "That wasn't God. They're crazy." There are millions of people in the world who look at Christians and say, "That's not God. You're crazy."

Now how do we know they're not right? This was a problem for me. It was a particularly vexing problem because I was in a religious tradition that was deeply invested in having everything right. And if I came to the conclusion it was not possible to get everything right, the question is, "Upon what is my relationship with God going to be based now since it has been based on getting it right. Am I going to lose myself?" Or the question we're asking at large, "Are we going to lose our heritage in Churches of Christ?" That was the problem.

The Solution Is Grace

So what is the solution? My solution in a word is this. Grace. And I'm perfectly comfortable with the old formulation. Grace. Grace. All is grace. I went through a long period of time where grace was relatively unimportant to me. And then you have that discovery that you're not quite as good at living this out as you thought you were. And (not to be not funny) I'm not good at it at all. I wish I were. When people write nasty things about me, what I think is, "If they only knew." So the notion that you don't have to do it all right to be in relationship with God became very precious to me. As it did to you. That it's not about perfection. It's about direction. However you want to say it. That God says "Yes" to me even when I'm not doing his will so well. That it's not by works lest any person should boast. And so I had come to this idea that grace extends to behavior.

That was the beginning of the step that was to save me. Not only do you not have to do it all right, you don't have to get it all right either. Why is it that we would believe that grace extends to behavior but doesn't extend to theology? Surely it can't be right that God is gracious in behavior but not in theology. To be a perfect theologian is the requisite for relationship with God? Boy, if it is, what a mess we're in! And so if I'm willing to accept God's grace in the realm of behavior, why can't I accept God's grace in the realm of conviction? God in his graciousness knows that I'm not always going to get it right. I believe that to the bottom of my toes and the middle of my bones and I hope I'm right about that. Because frankly, if I'm not, I think we're all going to hell. I don't know how to say it any straighter than that.

I run into so many brilliant, good, well-meaning people who give different answers to important theological questions. And if God turns out to be a fussy fault finder when it comes to theological ideas, all is lost.

That doesn't mean that right answers don't matter. It means we need a little humility. I want you to imagine a person who is right on every single issue. Every issue. She thinks God's thoughts after him on every issue. Except one. She's wrong on the instrumental music question. Now you see I very cleverly positioned myself where you don't know what her position is. Therefore you do not know what mine is. She's right on everything except that one. Do I really in my heart of hearts believe that because she is wrong on that one issue she had just as well be a member of the Church of Satan as a member of the Christian group she follows? I do not believe that for a moment. I don't. I don't think your relationship with God is based on getting it all right.

We do have new problems brewing among our youth who increasingly take the view that it's not important to get anything right. And I take that problem very seriously. I want to pay homage to my own discipline. I believe in biblical and theological scholarship. I think we should study the Bible more, not less. I think we should try harder, not less hard. I think we should be more rigorous in trying to get it right. Not less. But it is crucial at the end of the day that we acknowledge when we did our best we almost certainly didn't get it all right. By God's grace, that's okay.

My bias is that a little humility about what we know would solve a great many of the church fights we're currently having. When somebody comes after me and I get pushed to the wall, it often becomes so important to me to be right that I'll argue my position stronger than I know the evidence warrants. I get a feeling there are some other people who do that too. I know that there are many like me who had a great deal invested in having it all right. I know the comfort there is in that because I've experienced it.

But it's a dreadful burden. To continue to try hard to do our best with the mind that we have and still say at the end of the day, "Grace. Grace. All is Grace," is a liberating position. You don't have to give up your passion for God and your passion to come as close as you can to God's perfect will in order to be humbled about what you know. I think we'd be a better church and better people if we had that humility.

I don't know if my journey matches yours at all. I want to say to those who are younger that truth matters. It always matters. Be rigorous. Be committed. And I want to say to those older that humility matters. Be humble. Be prepared to admit that where you're located sometimes impacts the way you see things. Be ready to admit with me that disagreement with me is not necessarily disagreement with God. That's where I was. I thought when you disagreed with me, in my interpretation of Scripture, you were disagreeing with God because I was right. It may not turn out that way. Grace. Grace. All is Grace. What I've described to you is basically my postmodernism. That is, I am learning to make peace with a loss of certainty. And I'm doing that not by jumping into relativism, but by immersing myself in God's grace.

Chapter Six

THE EXPLOSION OF EXPERIENCE

I don't really like to have people sitting behind my back. In class, if I say, "Is that a llama behind you?" the students immediately look. And that's the way we figure out if there's really a llama there or not. Now in philosophy we have a word for that. That is called inter-subjective verifiability. I say, "Hey, is that a llama?" and you all look and say, "No, that's not a llama. That's a big dog." And I say, "Okay, it's a big dog." That's how we figure out if stuff is true or not.

So try this one. "I'm hot." Now you notice that is not inter-subjectively verifiable. Because whether I'm feeling hot or not doesn't have anything to do with how you're feeling. All married couples know how that works.

THE PROBLEM WITH EXPERIENCE

So the problem is that religious experiences by their very nature are not really inter-subjectively verifiable. Somebody will tell you about a wild religious experience and (depending on your personality type) you either believe them or not. But because they're telling you about their experience, there's no immediate way to verify it. And because of that, my heritage (and my education for that matter) taught me that experience was not to be trusted.

And there are so many ways to deceive yourself. I was suspicious about experience to start out with and then I read Freud. Then I was frightened. How do I know if I'm having some sort of experience of something out there or if I'm just having a spell? How do I know? I want something more reliable than that. Of course what was supposed to be more reliable than that (this is the laughable part) was my mind, because it's objective and it's reasonable and it's inter-subjectively verifiable.

But several things have happened. Culture has changed. I don't know if I like it or not, but that is really beside the point. Experience is more or less the coin of the realm now. Now this is particularly annoying to a reasonably good arguer. But I am more and more often having the experience of winning the argument and losing the person. I'm having more and more of this reaction from students when I try to get them into the argument. They give me the mantra of their generation: "Whatever." But it did set me to wondering if there is anything to this game they're playing.

Another thing happened. I went through a mid-life crisis. It was a real pain. Because the way I was going to go through my mid-life crisis was somewhat limited. I did not have a wife to divorce. Given my coordination, buying a motorcycle was just out of the question. So I moved to Texas. But that didn't help! What I was really experiencing is what my friend John of the Cross calls "the dark night of the soul." And what I was longing for was an experience of the God I said I believed in, a longing close to the heart of all believers who haven't stifled it completely.

How many of you have bungee jumped before? It is a rush. I mean, you're just free falling and then you're bouncing up and down looking at the world upside down. It is a glorious experience. Though, as I said earlier, I'm never doing it again. Now you didn't just have the experience. I told you about it, but you didn't have the experience. The real thing is completely different. It's scary. It's exhilarating. You can decide to protect yourself the rest of your life and not put yourself in a position to ever have a religious experience and pretend there's nothing to any of it, but I'm just telling you that if you do that you're going to miss an awful lot.

When you invite religious experience into your life there are two things that can happen. Both are bad. One is nothing. The other is something. Now think about it. Nothing is bad but sometimes something is worse. Because if you have a genuine religious experience, it makes demands on you. As you come to encounter the living God you have to take him seriously. And if you invite an experience of God, it is almost assured that he's going to mess with you in ways you don't yet know.

FROM HISTORY TO COMMITMENT

I've been reading John a good bit lately and it is a fascinating book. I've really gotten pulled into John's orbit here. One thing that's interesting to me about John is that it was probably written around 80 A.D., which essentially makes it a second generation document. In other words, John is probably the only gospel written to people who almost certainly had no firsthand experience with Jesus. Now that makes it an interesting read. When John tosses in little throwaway lines like "Blessed are you who have seen and believed but more blessed are those who haven't seen. . . ," he's doing something there. What do you say to Jewish people who are getting kicked out of the synagogues? That's my best guess at the setting of John.

That makes John 9 the centerpiece of the book. You remember the story. Jesus heals the man born blind, and his parents just wimp out on the whole situation because they're afraid they're going to get kicked out of the synagogue. John is writing to people who haven't had first-hand experience of Jesus. They're getting kicked out of the synagogues, and he's trying to give them this reassuring message about who Jesus really is and why they should hitch their wagon to Jesus. And in John we get this really interesting doctrine on the Holy Spirit. John does this stuff on the Holy Spirit that we don't see in the synoptics.

Let me show you one place—John 16:

Now I am going to him who sent me, yet none of you asks me, "Where are you going?" Because I have said these things, you are filled with grief. But I tell you the truth: It is for your good that I am going away. Unless I go away, the Counselor will not come to you; but if I go, I will send him to you. When he comes, he will convict the world of

guilt in regard to sin and righteousness and judgment: in regard to
sin, because men do not believe in me; in regard to righteousness,
because I am going to the Father, where you can see me no longer;
and in regard to judgment, because the prince of this world now
stands condemned.   JOHN 16:5-11

This is really the only passage that talks about the Holy Spirit having any
relationship with people who are not Christian. And that relationship is primarily one of judgment. I hear teaching on the Holy Spirit that seems to go into a
different direction, where the notion is the Holy Spirit is operating on the person
outside of Christ to bring them to faith, but John doesn't quite say that.

I have much more to say to you, more than you can now bear. But
when he, the Spirit of truth, comes, he will guide you into all truth.
He will not speak on his own; he will speak only what he hears, and he
will tell you what is yet to come. He will bring glory to me by taking
from what is mine and making it known to you. All that belongs to
the Father is mine. That is why I said the Spirit will take from what is
mine and make it known to you.

    In a little while you will see me no more, and then after a little
while you will see me.   JOHN 16:12-16

I'm going to tell you what I think John is doing. I'm going to give you a
little spiritual autobiography. How do you move from a historical probability
to a life of commitment? The vast majority of you readers believe in the bodily
resurrection of Jesus Christ. I can give you some historical evidence for that
conviction. But the best I can do with any piece of history is create a level of
probability. Because history is not science. History is made up of one-of-a-
kind events. How do you prove something is true in science? Well, what you
do is keep doing it. It's reproducible.

    So at one point we had these guys in Utah who claimed to have done cold
fusion but nobody else could do it and they couldn't do it again. So what do we
conclude? They didn't do it. But history is not like that. History is one-of-a-kind

events. And so we rely on things like physical evidence and testimony and even circumstantial evidence; with it we can establish things with various levels of probability. There are some things that I can establish with such a high level of probability I will say I know it happened. What I'm saying is, "I think there's a very high level of probability this happened."

For instance, Lincoln gave the Gettysburg address. I believe that with great probability. I'm a little more dubious about George Washington and that cherry tree thing. I don't have quite as high a level of probability. I had this aunt who was never totally convinced that people walked on the moon. She thought they had faked that one for some sinister purpose we were never entirely clear about. Now again, that's one I think I could establish with a relatively high level of probability. I'm still talking about probability here. I'm not too convinced about the Elvis sightings in 7-11 stores. I can't totally rule this out. It's just so charming. Who would want to totally rule it out? It gives you a purpose to live—to roam the earth hoping to have an Elvis sighting.

Now where does the bodily resurrection of Jesus Christ stand on that continuum? It is somewhere between Elvis at the 7-11 and the Gettysburg address. Are you with me? Now depending on the historian you talk to, we could have a debate about how more or less probable it is. But wherever you put it, what you're going to be talking about is probability. Now the question is why would I stake my life and give my undying commitment to a historical probability? And I think John's answer is because of the present witness of the Holy Spirit. The Holy Spirit is the continuing presence of God that testifies in us to the resurrection of Jesus Christ.

On the first day of my freshman Bible major class on the life and teachings of Christ I ask them the following question, "Do you believe in the living Lord because of the resurrection or do you believe in the resurrection because of the living Lord?" If I ask you that question, those of you who know me well know the right answer. "Yes." And my feeling is that's the way faith works. It's not like the historical evidence doesn't mean anything. It's just that it's not everything. There's also the continuing witness of the living Lord that confirms the historical evidence.

That's what John is doing. That's why I am concerned if we do not have a doctrine of the Spirit. The Spirit is God's continuing presence among his people. That makes experience very important. But we have the little problem I started out with in the beginning which is that religious experience is not inter-subjectively verifiable, so we've always got questions about how we confirm it. You could decide just not to go bungee jumping at all. You could stay off the tower. But you miss a lot. Let me say a word or two about my own experience and then talk about discernment a bit.

An Experience of God

I didn't really want a spectacular experience. I just wanted one. I'd go and read Habakkuk 2:20: "The Lord is in his holy temple. Let all the earth keep silence before him." That verse comes at the end of a discussion of idol worship. He's talking about how foolish it is to speak to an idol and he says, when it comes to the living God, you should be silent because he's in his holy temple. So I'm wondering. Maybe I don't ever have an experience of God because I'm being so loud he can't get through.

So I go on my own little field trip to do original research in the existence of God. One does not do this in the library. One does it in the desert. I had a friend who said, "There's this great place down in South Texas. You ought to go down there some time. I went down there to pray and it's really a great place. There are these hermits down there and you'll really like it." And he sent me their website.

Now that already had my head spinning. What on earth is a hermit doing with a website? What is this world coming to! So I looked at it and it looked like an interesting place, but what caught my eye was that they had a 40-day wilderness program where you did 40 days of silent prayer. I couldn't get it out of my mind. For the next six months I couldn't think of anything else. I wondered what would happen if I gave God my undivided attention for 40 days. I started taking tentative little steps. I started clearing my schedule. So now I had the time and I had the money and the only thing that was holding me back was I couldn't decide whether I wanted to do that or not. I even visited the place for a couple of days. I felt safe there. I felt good. I thought two things could happen and they're both bad. Nothing and something.

So I started to bargain with God. "Okay, I'll go, God, but don't mess with me." Now this is where my friends, such are they are, were not helpful. They would say stuff like, "Yeah, you're going to get out there and God's going to tell you to get married." You know. "God is going to call you to Madagascar." All that stuff. And then there were the family and friends who just couldn't even understand the notion.

"What are you going to do for 40 days?"

"Nothing. I want to pray for 40 days."

"What are you going to pray about for 40 days? You can pray for everybody in the whole wide world and then what do you do?"

"I'm not going to ask for anything, I'm just going to go. I'm going to go be quiet and see if the Lord is in his holy temple or not."

So I went. And you know the first problem was decompression. I live my life at a faster pace than I should, so the first thing was just trying to get used to the idea that there was nothing to do. I was pacing. I've got to do something. And it was hot. They didn't have air conditioning. They've got a website but no air conditioning. So I'm thinking, "What am I going to do here in my little dwelling for the next 40 days?" I said, "Okay, breathe deep, you can do this. Let's see what we're doing here."

I had all of these ridiculous notions about what would happen. I really believed that something like the following might happen. For the first 30 or 35 days it would be nothing. God would be testing my commitment. I'm remembering my friends again. They would say, "What if you get out there and after 20 days you can't stand it anymore?" I said I would pack up my car and I would go. They said, "You can do that?" And I said, "It's a hermit community, not a concentration camp. You know, they don't have people sitting up there on the barbed wire ready to mow you down if you try to leave."

I thought, I'm going to be there for 30 to 35 days, God is going to see my good heart, my great intentions, and then one day when I'm walking down one of the paths he's going to meet me at the end of the path and say, "Okay, I believe you're for real. Sit down here and let's talk." I would first of all ask him the serious and vocational questions I had and we would move from there to the difficult texts of the Bible. I would say, "What did you mean by that one?" And we would clear it all up and I would leave to bestow this knowledge on a waiting world.

That didn't happen. It's a romantic idea. It's a tedious experience. The food was the same everyday. It was hot. I would get bored on Thursdays. There was something about Thursday. Part of it was like Andy Griffith. After supper I would sit on the porch and rock. Because there was nothing to do. It was tedious. It was beyond tedious. At the beginning, it was simply miserable. Because I found out that being noisy is a wonderful way not to have to deal with your life. When you lose words, which is the primary way I cast the vision of myself that I want you to see, and you're stuck there before God in his holiness, you discover what Isaiah discovered: "Woe is me. I am a man of unclean lips."

All the woundedness and crud and sin in my life rushed to the surface. I've read enough in the tradition to know this is pretty common experience. It's not just mine. I didn't know what to do about it. I got some good advice from a hermit. It is slightly more difficult getting information out of a hermit than it is out of a spy.

I said, "I don't know what to do here. I don't know if this is me. I don't know if this is God. I don't know if this is Satan. I don't like it."

But sometimes finding the right image is all you need. So the hermit said, "This is like smoke going out of a chimney. If you want to, you can try to put the lid on it but all you're going to do is drive the smoke back down into the house. That is what you've been doing all these years. I suppose you could obsess over it."

I said, "No, I don't want to do that."

He says, "Then let it go."

I had taught salvation by grace in my classes in often eloquent ways. When I was really on, I could even make students cry. But it was in the desert that I had the experience of coming to understand that God loves me just the way I am. And it slipped from my head to my heart. It wasn't spectacular. I'll tell you in a little while why I think it was real.

After a while I got where I enjoyed being out there. After I got past that crud section it was cool. I would go out and I would be on the trail praying and there would be no hurry to get back because when I got back there was nothing to do. This is the only time in my life when this has been true. Even now when I set aside long times for prayer I often find myself thinking about what comes after. But there were no distractions because there was nothing to do. It got really comfortable and I got where I liked to rock on the porch.

I began to hear in my head God's call to me to be a hermit. I thought, "This is it. This is what I'm called to do. The eremitical lifestyle. I finally have found myself." But this thought did pose certain problems. The Churches of Christ are not quite as well equipped as I wish they were to support the hermit's lifestyle. That tends to be more of a Catholic thing. But I had a plan. I've made a lot of friends in churches and I would just to go a church and say, "Would you please support my ministry?"

And they would say, "We would love to; what is your ministry?"

"I want to be a hermit."

"Okay, what do hermits do?"

"Nothing."

And they would say, "We would like to help you but we've already got two guys on staff doing that."

I thought I'd eventually find a church to support me. But here I am. It's pretty obvious that I decided that wasn't my call.

WAIT AND DISCERN

My story makes an important point about religious experience. I stress to my students that not every nudge you feel is God's Holy Spirit. Not every good idea you have comes from God. You've got to learn to be discerning. Sometimes you've got to wait. You've got to be patient. You've got to submit your ideas to God and to the church. I really believe in communal discernment. I think communal discernment is about the only way one can protect oneself from one's own idiosyncrasy. You submit it to spiritual people that you trust and who submit it back to prayer, because not everything you feel is God's movement.

As I got ready to leave after the 40 days it was with mixed feelings. On the one hand, I was anxious to get back to my church. I was anxious to get back to my dogs. I was anxious to get back to my students. I was anxious to get back to M & Ms. On the other hand, all I could think was that when I get to school there are going to be 500 emails waiting. And some of them are going to require a response. My friends refer to me as the Dead Sea of e-mail. I receive and I receive but I do not give.

My first stop on my way out of the hermit's community was Wal-Mart. I think I walked around in a daze because it seemed so noisy. There were people talking all the time. But as I was leaving I just had this overwhelming under-standing that the living God was going with me. That he's a God not just of the desert, but he's the God of everyday life. And that if one was attentive, one could continue to experience his presence.

My experience isn't a pattern for anybody else's. But I cannot tell you how much it has meant to my own faith in life to allow religious experience back in the house. I want to encourage you to be open to that. To confirm your con-victions about the resurrection by placing yourself in a position to experience the living Lord. The question is whether we are willing to cultivate the ground and then be discerning about what we experience. Some of you apparently are not wired this way and so you're going to stay off the bungee tower. That's fine. But if you want to let the experience of God become a part of your life, you have to cultivate the ground. My students driven by experience unfortu-nately do not desire to practice the disciplines in a way that will allow them to have the experience of God they truly want. And the alternatives to that are to manufacture it or imagine it or to say there's nothing to it.

POSTMODERN MYSTICISM

My love/hate relationship with worship renewal in Churches of Christ is well known. To be sure, we've needed some worship renewal among us, but it bothers me that it often looks so frantic. As if a little more excitement, a little more noise, a little more activity will somehow convince us that God is in our midst. Maybe that's the wrong direction. Maybe the Lord is in his holy temple and so we should get silent before him.

I cannot and will not, because it would be both unethical and unchristian, pass judgment on anyone else's claim to religious experience. But if we want a genuine experience of the living God the way is more likely to be found along the path of the traditional spiritual disciplines than along any other path. Because Scripture and 2000 years of Christian history testify to them. And as we follow the great saints of history down that path, God keeps his promises and we experience the living Lord. Not always in spectacular ways. Not usually in spectacular ways.

Since I've come back from the hermit's community I engage in contemplative prayer ten hours a week. What happens? Most of the time, nothing. I'm just spending time with the one I love. Do I get revelations? No. I wish I did. Visions? No. Wish I did. Revelation on what you should do on some particular decision? No, not so far. Hoping for that one. But no. Experience of the living God over time? Absolutely. If I make myself available, God comes to meet me there. And so I think commitment to preparing the ground so we can hear God and perceive God and experience God is the human part. And then we try to trust God to do what he said he would do.

I've told many of you my favorite story about Albert Einstein. He is teaching in some university and he's getting ready to give a final test. And his graduate assistant says, "Mr. Einstein you cannot give this test."

And he says, "Why not?"

And the assistant says, "Because you gave this test last year."

Einstein says, "So?"

The assistant says, "You've got to understand about students. They keep files. And even though this is a complicated test, there would have been students assigned last year to memorize the different portions of this test and they will be reproduced and passed on to this group of students and the students are going to know all of the questions on this test."

And Einstein says, "It doesn't matter. All the answers are different this year."

I can believe in science that could happen. My conviction is in theology it ought not to. Since Scripture and 2000 years of history have said, "This is the way that you have a genuine experience of God," then we ought to wake up and pay attention and try that path. So now you know why I am a postmodern mystic. One who believes that God could be encountered, not just in Scripture, not just in nature, but in the quiet of the desert.

Chapter Seven

THE EXPLOSION OF PRESENCE

One of the really difficult issues of my own theological life—and I'm
convinced of the theological life of most—is to try to understand
how God works in the world, especially in instances where he doesn't seem
to be doing as well as he might. And for those of us who experience intensely
calling upon God and getting nothing out of it, those who tell how God is
answering every prayer that they are praying become intensely annoying. In
fact, they can become absolutely faith threatening. Because while the elder in
my church is dying and the whole church is coming together in deep prayer
for healing, somebody else is talking about how they couldn't find a parking
place and they prayed to God and (lo and behold) one opened up. And I think,
what is this? God does parking? He doesn't do elders?

Most of you remember the event of the near miraculous (I mean this
facetiously) rescue of those miners a few years ago and the praises to God that
went for that. I'm wondering why God let them get in that mess in the first
place. You would think if he could rescue them, he could have kept them from
digging into that water-filled shaft in the first place. I keep wondering what
people would have been saying if they had all died. It looked to me as if the
rescue came from remarkable acts of human courage, human resourcefulness,

some good luck, and some crucially right decisions. I don't know about God. Because while those miners are being rescued, a baby in my church is dying of cancer. Are we less faithful when we call to God for healing and get nothing out of it? It really makes you wonder what God's doing in the world, doesn't it?

Biblical Panentheism

I want to stake out a pretty clear position. I'm not a Calvinist. I do not think that everything happens in the world directly because God has caused it or desired it. I'm tempted to suggest that that makes God a monster. Nor am I a deist. I'm not one of those who think God wound up the world and hasn't done much of anything since the closing of the last book of the Bible. What I am instead is a panentheist, which is one who believes that in all things God is working—in death as well as life, in sickness as well as health, in disaster as well as rescue.

I want you to look at what I think is one of the truly difficult texts in the Bible, 2 Samuel 12. David has gotten into his mess with Bathsheba and (as is usually the case in politics) the cover-up has made the crime even worse. We have this beautifully provocative text where Nathan comes and confronts David. "Then David said to Nathan, 'I have sinned against the Lord.' Nathan replied, 'The Lord has taken away your sin, you are not going to die, but because by doing this you have made the enemies of the Lord show utter contempt—the son born to you will die.'"

Does that text bother you a little? What is God doing here? Here's my best guess. God says you're not going to die. I think there's a parenthesis there: even though you deserve to. My own opinion is that God wants to kill David. David deserves to die. But the reason God is not going to kill David is because David is carrying the promise of the covenant. To overstate it a little, God can't kill David. So he says, "I'm going to preserve the covenant but I'm going to kill your baby." This baby is not going to die of natural causes. My first inclination is to think, "What a tough God." But then I have another inclination. In this horrid story, God finds a way. He finds a way to preserve the covenant. In these most horrid events, God finds a way because God works in all things.

I don't think God caused David to sin with Bathsheba or kill Uriah. That was all David. What is remarkable is that God looks at that mess and he found a way. He always finds a way.

A guy retired recently from IBM. He is one of my heroes because he wrote the program for control-alternate-delete, the command to re-boot computers. Wrote it in 15 minutes. I do not know what his religious commitments are, but the man is going to heaven. I've often thought that is the way life ought to work. Give me a little control-alternate-delete in my life. Let me just re-boot everything and start all over. You ever have those moments? David wants to do control-alternate-delete and he can't. He's created this mess that will haunt his kingdom forever, but God finds a way. He always finds a way.

One of my favorite Old Testament books is Esther, where some serious weirdness is going on. I don't know what to make of it. I think it's supposed to be funny. I think most things are. You can go ahead and look at life as a drama if you want to. It's a lot more interesting if you look at it as farce. There is this crazy book of Esther and I don't know what to do with it. It's like good news and bad news. Here's the bad news. The king is an idiot. He throws a drunken party. Calls his queen to come out and show his friends what a comely queen she is. The good news is the queen is virtuous and won't display herself. The bad news is the king fires her. But the good news is the king's going to pick another queen. And it's going to be Esther. And I don't know if you've noticed, but God is nowhere in sight.

The bad news is the king is an idiot. He passes an irrevocable decree that all the Jews are to be killed. The good news is Mordecai finds out about it and the Jews have an inside person, Queen Esther. The bad news is she doesn't really want this job. The good news is Mordecai is very persuasive. The bad news is there is this bad guy, Haman, hanging around the king. Haman erects the gallows on which he wishes to kill Mordecai. It's 75 feet high. You know what you call that? Overkill.

But the good news is the king has insomnia. He's reading a book of all the happenings at court (that should put him to sleep). He finds that Mordecai at one point has done him a great turn, so he wants to do something for

Mordecai. And the good news is the queen screws up her courage to go in front of the king and he holds out the scepter and she's going to throw him another party. It's good news. The good news is that the queen is sneaky. At the beginning of the book she looks a little like a valley girl, but at the end she's looking like Mata Hari. She sets Haman up. He gets killed. Good news. I don't know if you've noticed God is nowhere in sight.

Well, there is some more bad news, I guess. The king is an idiot. He's passed this irrevocable decree that all the Jews are to be killed and he can't revoke it so what he does is he passes another one that says the Jews can defend themselves. So this idiot of a king sets up a situation where all of his subjects get to kill each other. But this turns out to be good news. The Jews win. I don't know if you've noticed, but God is still nowhere in sight. Don't you love that book?

In a lot of ways, Esther is the book for our time. I've got to believe (I don't know, maybe it's my personality) that the writer the whole time is going wink, wink, nod, nod. God's nowhere in sight. Surely we're supposed to see here that the God who's nowhere in sight is everywhere. I believe through a whole lot of our lives that God is nowhere in sight. He actually prefers the shadows to the light.

Even in the Old Testament where we think God is doing something all the time, it doesn't seem to be true. Look at poor Abraham. God basically gives him a direct appearance three times and every time something terrible happens. Every time God shows up Abraham is probably saying, "Oh no. Not again. I had to move. I've been raising teenagers when I'm a hundred. That sacrifice thing was no fun." What was Abraham thinking when he was walking up Mount Moriah to sacrifice Isaac? Listening, listening, listening for the voice of God, but all around was silence.

In the same way preaching begins where God is silent. That's right, isn't it? If God wasn't silent we wouldn't have preaching. We would just all listen to God. I believe that God is in all things. Now I want to be pretty careful theologically with what I'm doing here. This is not a Calvinist stance; I don't think God is doing everything in the world. I think God is trying to do something *with* everything in the world. And that's not the same thing. And I think that's what Romans 8:28 is saying. That "in all things God is working for the good of those who love him." If you'll look at the end of Romans 8 you'll see it takes this eschatological trajectory. What it tells us is the whole world is groaning in travail waiting for redemption. But that eventually God is going to take this travail and turn it into a baby.

One of my really fine preaching students really grabbed hold of this notion (it was one of those sermons when after it's preached you don't grade it, you just steal it). He's doing this sermon for me on Abraham and Sarah's long wait for Isaac to come along. It's such a creative sermon because he takes Sarah's side. He points out that Sarah is waiting for God to do his thing and God is not getting anything done. So Sarah does the Hagar thing and tries to help God along in a way that cuts her completely out of the picture. And then (in the greatest line in the sermon) he points out it is really hard to deal with a God who has no concept of time. Now that's great. That's worth an "A." Because for a lot of us the question is not how, the question is not why, the question is when. When, oh Lord?

GOD WORKS IN GOOD AND BAD

I want to talk for just a few minutes about what I think is a really cancerous theology. A deadly theology. That is our inclination to see God working in every good thing and not working in the bad stuff. I think that flies in the face of Scripture and (if we really thought about it) flies in the face of our own experience. I want to argue that God is working in all things, even in the darkness. In Gethsemane, where Jesus is not getting what he's asking for, in that moment God is working.

I'm looking for God everywhere and that has its own dangers. It wouldn't do to be presumptive about this. It is never good to be too sure about what God is doing in the world. I will repeat, for those of you who haven't heard it yet, the two kinds of Christians you cannot trust: the ones who think God is doing nothing and the ones who think they know exactly what God is doing. It's always presumptive to claim to know exactly what God is doing in the world other than this one thing: moving all things to the point where every knee will bow and every tongue will confess that Jesus is Lord.

I've been getting trained for the last couple of years in spiritual direction from a bunch of mystics. And spiritual direction is very different from pastoral counseling. Pastoral counseling is where you come in with a problem and I fix it. Let's put it another way. Pastoral counseling is where I listen to you for God's sake. Spiritual direction is where I listen to God for your sake. So when a person comes for spiritual direction the question I want to ask is what do you think God's doing here? What does God want to do with this?

It is especially important to ask that question where things aren't going at all the way you wish. It is easy to be glib about what God is doing when everything is coming up roses. It's another thing to ask the hard questions. What is it that's happening here? What is God trying to do? There are some things I like to point out to my students about the bad things that happen in the world. If God had intended the world to be Disneyland then the world surely is a dismal failure, but that only counts as a failure if that's what God intended to do. The example I give them is my really cool pen. This is a great pen because I can click it closed and I can put it in my pocket and if I have my pants on I always have a pen. And when you're as absent minded as I am that helps your chances. I have from time to time needed to do other things with it. There was a screw loose on my glasses. Let me tell you, this pen will not help that. It won't. I have discovered the pen is a lousy screwdriver. But it is a good pen.

So if the world was intended to be a place of nothing but ongoing wonderful delightful pleasures, then we have to give God an "F" on it. But maybe that's not what the world is. Maybe the world is the place where we can learn to be children to God and brothers and sisters to our fellow human beings. I would argue the world works very well doing that. In many cases the most important lessons we learn are ones we would never have signed up for in the first place. And so we believe, that even in those things God works. Guess what I'm trying to convince you of? That God is on your side. The point of this Romans passage is to tell us that even when awful things happen in the world and God is nowhere in sight, God is looking to find a way. He's going to bring it into the plan. He's going to move all things towards redemption. That's what God does and he's good at it.

Sometimes God has to work in our spiritual meltdowns. Some of us have such a glib view of God that things have to happen to kill that view so that a truer and better view of God can take its place. And that's not always a real pleasant experience. I often get one of those people who say, "I just can't believe in God anymore," and I say, "No, no, no.......what you can't believe in is the God you believed in before. And thank God for that because that God wasn't God. This is an opportunity to find the true and living God, not the one you just so glibly took for granted earlier." And in that God works.

Here's the danger. This can be a way to protect ourselves from ever being disappointed in God. We can create a false picture. God is working in all things, so when things really go well that means it's God and when things are really going badly that means it's God. So there's never any reason to be disappointed in God or wonder about God. I don't want to take us there. I think the Psalms are instruction in high expectations of God. When you have high expectations of God and he doesn't always operate the way you think he's going to, you're going to have some disappointments. And I'll grant you that's a dicey world. Those of you who have read Psalms know it. You have those Psalm 88 moments. You say, "Oh God! God! God!!!" You can take a view of life where you never have those moments, but I don't want to go there.

When I was the president of the faculty senate at Lipscomb University, I very early developed a theme for my administration. "Low expectations, few disappointments." That's the way a lot of us deal with God. Our expectations are so low that we are never disappointed. I don't want to do that. I want us to pray believing God answers. I want us to expect God to interact with us in the world. I want us to be brave enough to call upon him when he doesn't seem to be coming through. I want us to be bold enough to badger God when he seems reluctant. To cry to God when he seems to have left the field. But when we've done all that, we look one more time and say, "Okay, God didn't do what I wanted. He didn't do what I expected. He didn't do what I thought he would do. But God always finds a way, so what's he doing?" When we ask that, life becomes full and interesting.

JOINING GOD'S WORK

I close with this point about mission. I am fairly intimidated by a great many sinners. I am particularly intimidated by 19-year-old sinners. I mean, those tough guys scare me to death. And I am really feeling a great desire to get into their world somehow and try to minister to them. Because right now at ACU I have a ministry to two groups of people: Bible majors that I do pretty well with, and searchers that I do pretty well with. I've got people who have real faith problems and care enough to come and talk them out. I do okay.

But there's this whole other group of people out there who are not Bible majors and they are not searchers. They are annoying. They are irritating sinners. And they have zero interest. I want to enter that world. I've been asking some of my students, "How do I get in that world?" And they say, "You're going to have to learn to play poker." I thought, "Oh man, this is going to be more costly than I had thought." So I said, "Okay. You teach me. I'll learn and for the sake of the kingdom of God if I have to go over at midnight and get into a poker game with a bunch of people I don't like, that's what I'm going to do."

Now, I only mildly enjoy preaching to people who really want to hear. So here I am. How am I going to be involved with these students? This is the only way I'm going to be able to do it. I'm going to believe that before I step foot there, God's already there. He's already working and I didn't have to recruit him to this agenda. All I had to do is show up where's he's already doing work. I may not be able to see it. My guess is I won't. I've looked pretty hard. I said, "Boy, God, your work is really subtle with that guy. It's hard to see that you are doing anything." But I believe he is. When I'm talking to the students struggling with their faith, I've got to believe this. I've got to believe that God's gotten there first. Because I'm not that smart. I don't have the right buttons to push. I don't have the right levers to pull. I have to believe God's there first. I'm like you. When I'm going to the funeral home, I have to believe God got there first. He's already working. I'm going to join him in his work. So that's my definition of panentheism. One who believes that God is working in all things.

I'm a postmodern, mystic, panentheist. Happily situated in Churches of Christ. And I am going nowhere. You can be a postmodern, mystic, panentheist and be perfectly happy in this tradition. For one thing there is so much meaningful work to do. I just say to myself, "Where else would I be so desperately needed?" We are not nearly as carbon-copy groups of people as some make us out to be. We have a great variety in our churches. So this is my plea. Don't leave. Our tradition is so greatly enriched by people who don't all see it exactly the same way. We need those who are driven by the mind and those who are driven by the heart, those who are given to Christian activity and those who are given to prayer and contemplation, those who are given to quiet and those who are given to raucous enthusiasm, those who are constantly joyful and those of us who are slightly depressed. We need them all, because in all of these people, God works to move things to the final glorious conclusion when God will be all in all.

SECTION III

Navigating the Brave New World

Chapter Eight

LIFE AFTER THE DEATH OF HUMANITY

When people came to Jesus and wanted to know more about him, he did not preach them a sermon. He did not have classes and give lectures. He did not argue or write books. He simply said, "Come and see." He invited them to follow him into a completely new world, the world that God always intended. He called it the kingdom of God.

However, for centuries his followers (who think they know more than he does) have preached and argued and lectured and taught people into being Christians. None of that seems to work much anymore. We are living in a world where those old certainties have died. Good riddance. Perhaps our world is ready again for another approach. The way of Jesus. The way of "Come and follow."

If we are wiling to take him seriously and really follow him, then we become part of a new humanity. The promise of a bright new world with which the technological age began has pretty much crashed. Technology has not made us more human or humane, and there does seem to have been the death, if not of humanity, at least of basic civility. What Christianity proclaims is a new humanity. What would it look like to experience this new humanity in a world of shattered dreams about what humans could be? I'm going to identify seven characteristics of a new humanity and lay them over against our human experience at the moment.

Absolute Calm

One of the characteristics of the new humanity is *shalom* in a frantic and anxious world. That is, the new humanity is marked by absolute calm. Christian people ought to be the most serene people you know. How you doing on that one? I don't know if you've noticed, but we live in a frantic and anxious world. What we often do in our churches is invite people to become a bit more that way. That is, they now have all the things they had before to worry about before they were Christians plus a few more. That shouldn't be what happens.

Where does this *shalom* come from? It comes from knowing how things turn out. You have feelings of peace and calm because you know in the end when sin and sickness, disease and death, war and plague, and the devil himself have done their worst, God has the last word. That drives this frantic anxiety out of our lives so we're then able to abide in what Scripture calls *shalom* or peace.

I'm primarily talking about inner peace, although I do think it would be reflected in a lack of hostility in the world. I am struck that almost everybody in the world, including Christians, seems to be extraordinarily angry. It doesn't take anything to set us off. Once we understand where God is taking the world, the stuff that is ordinarily anxiety producing loses a lot of its hold on us, because (to put it in a really cliché sort of way) this too will pass. It all does. You need to think about whether things pass the eternity test or not. Do they matter for the long haul? Most of the things that produce conflict and anxiety in our churches and in our lives won't even pass the ten-minute test, much less the eternity test.

Now being one of those fearful and anxious people myself, I do understand that. I try to keep my students from being like I was. I used to think that whether I made an "A" in class was really important. And now my task is to convince my students it doesn't matter. I say, "Do you really think anybody will care thirty years from now whether you made an 'A' or a 'B' in my class? I don't think anybody will care six weeks from now." And they say, "Well, if that's the case, just give us the higher grade." You know people who have this *shalom* and you want to be around them. They're the people who, when they come into the room, make everything calmer because they have a sense of proportion. They don't get pulled into drama.

SELF AWARENESS

The second characteristic of the new humanity is we have self awareness in a posturing world. That is, we know who we are and we have neither too high nor too low a view of ourselves. So we have no need to pose or to posture. We live in a world where posturing is a way of life. We teach our students to do this. It's called resumé writing. We want you to posture. We want you to put your best face forward. But self awareness leads to the most elusive of all Christian virtues that we call humility. When we really understand who we are, there is no room to posture because we understand that before God we have nothing to claim.

It's hard to figure out how to get humility. The pursuit of it is one sure way not to get it because then you have the pride of having achieved humility and you don't have it anymore. The only way you can get humility is by indirection. Humility is what happens while you're doing or pursuing something else. In that way it's very much like happiness. One sure way not to be happy is to pursue happiness. Happiness is what happens while you're pursuing some other things.

So I started reading people who wrote on humility. That takes some nerve, doesn't it? I relate to the guy who said, "You know, I used to be conceited, but now I'm perfect and I don't have that problem either." Read the Rule of St. Benedict. It's the basic rule for all monastic life and somewhere in there he gives steps toward humility. They are really interesting. They are very culturally bound. Some of them are just annoying. For instance, St. Benedict has no room for humor. No frivolous speech at all. But he talks about ways that you can find your way into humility.

Another who has written brilliantly on this is Jeremy Taylor who's got all these rules for being humble. I don't know how many of them there are. A lot. And some of them again are odd, but a lot of them just catch you. He says, "Don't belittle yourself in front of other people in the hopes that they will say, 'No, No, No, that's not true.'" And when they notice that you really are of no account, you should be grateful that they have helped you realize your position before God. He says, "Never get into a conversation that you try to steer in a way that will make you look good, or make you the center of the conversation."

I wonder what the world would be like if in the new humanity we took seriously our hopeless position before God. If we quit posturing and quit trying to acquire power and influence because we really do understand it's all empty. And then I wonder what would happen if we realized that even in that circumstance, when we were without hope, Christ died for us. All of a sudden I can breathe and I don't have to try to pretend to be somebody to you that I'm not, because we're all in the same mess and we're all saved by the same gracious act of God. If I'm understanding what's happening in Romans, that's what Paul is trying to do to solve this Jew/Gentile problem. He's trying to convince both Jews and Gentiles that they are equally damned and both equally saved and so they should quit posturing with one another. You don't have to do that, even in a world where we are so desperate to impress and to gain influence. I like the term "self awareness" because this is not a matter of convincing ourselves of anything. This is just a matter of recognizing our position before God.

Open to the Other

Number three. The new humanity is open and nonjudgmental in a tribal world. We live in a world that traffics in "us and them." It tries to set us up as "us and them" in a variety of ways. It creates gender warfare. It creates class warfare. It creates ethnic warfare. It creates religious sectarian warfare. It creates righteous-versus-sinner warfare.

Now when I was talking about being nonjudgmental I'm not suggesting that we don't make any sort of judgments in the world. That would be ridiculous. What I am suggesting is that we epitomize the new humanity in the way that Jesus did. And he is open to everybody. He seems remarkably comfortable with everybody. This is one of those characteristics I would really like to have. I would like to be like Jesus and be able to go into rich people's homes and eat their food and not be intimidated and mooch off their generosity, then go to the party of the tax collectors and the prostitutes and be equally comfortable there. I'd like to go to the temple and be comfortable and then go to Samaria and be comfortable with the sinful Samaritan woman. I wonder what it would be like to be that open and nonjudgmental presence in the world.

The call to prophetic ministry is important, but prophetic ministry so easily ceases to be a word for God and becomes instead a word of attack and oppression. I am quick to see the sin and the problems in everybody's lives and not so quick to see the Christ who is trying to be formed in them. I don't know how to do that.

But I do know that the tribalism of the world has brought us to the brink of disaster. And at the moment our only antidote to tribalism is power. We have a case study going on in Iraq now where we discovered that the only thing holding the religious tribalism of Iraq in place was raw, oppressive, torturous power. And the moment that power is removed, guess what? Tribalism is still there. Shiite and Sunni dislike each other more that either of them dislike us. How are we going to get this tribalism back under control? More power. Here Scripture comes in with this other notion, saying, "Instead of trying power why don't you try openness, not judgmentalism?"

Regard for Others

Four. A characteristic of the new humanity is regard for others in a narcissistic world. We might call this by the term "love." Love is such a gooey word. Last year in chapel at ACU they scheduled me to speak on Valentine's Day. And so I decided to speak directly to the guys. I said, "I know what you have been doing today. You have been shopping for the perfect Valentine. And this is perilous business. Because it has to say enough to let the girl know you really like her, but you must be really careful it doesn't say too much. Because then you're dead. You get her something silly, and she's going to dump you. But you get her something that says too much and boy are you tangled up then. Keep looking for the one that says just enough: 'I love you in a way that is going to keep you in my life in ways that I want but not in ways that complicate my own.'" Now that sounds like love, but when you analyze it, it's just a little bit narcissistic.

A recent study says the current generation of young people is the most narcissistic ever. They are very self absorbed. Now I don't know where they got it. They were maybe just hatched that way. But boy we've got problems here. The problem is that the whole world revolves around me. The primary symbol of this is the cell phone, which says you are so important that you can never be out of contact for a single moment or the world may fall apart. So in class you've got to be connected. I'm teaching the class and I've got students text messaging each other from across the room. I'm teaching and they're holding a conversation. In chapel, in church. It doesn't matter. I occasionally say to my students, "Do you know that the cell phone is a relatively new invention? Somehow we managed without it for hundreds of years." We have a problem here. We live in a world where it's all about me. It's about my comfort. It's about my desires. It's about my way. And even when we appear to be serving or caring for other people, we end up primarily serving ourselves.

What would it be like to really have regard for the other? If I'm understanding what Jesus is doing, he's trying to epitomize this for us. He's trying to show us what it means to care about other people, what it means to love. Is the command to love one another, found in the book of 1 John, a new command or an old command? Yes. I'll give you that it's an old command, but it's a new command. And the reason it's a new command is because it is now epitomized in Jesus. What's new about it is that we now see what this looks like. This is what it means to really have regard for the other.

We have developed a whole vocabulary to describe narcissistic behavior. We have words like passive aggressive. I don't like passive aggressive. My approach to life is aggressive aggressive. And I prefer that, because at least you know where you stand. I found myself giving instructions to some of my mentoring group the other day about how to manipulate a group. Let me give you a basic rule of group dynamics. When they're fighting you, give it over to them and then they'll start fighting for your position. I've done this a hundred times in an academic community where professors are trained to find what's wrong with your proposal. They don't have any proposals. That's not what they're trained to do. They're trained to critique yours. When they can't make it in the academy, they go become elders. I've been in a situation in a church where I'm trying to get something done that's not going anywhere and I finally say, "Okay, this was my bad. I thought we were ready to do this. I thought we had reached the point of maturing and discussion where we were ready to do this. But I was obviously wrong. We need to forget this. There's just no way we can do this." And the first thing they'll say is, "No, no, wait a minute." And pretty soon they're trying to talk me into my position. Is that cool or what?

No, that is not cool. It looks like I'm paying attention to the concerns of others, but what I'm really doing is using their concerns to get my way. I wonder what would happen if we started to take the point of view that the point is to lose? If we thought the point of the game was to get the fewest points, then I think we would become very competitive in that area. What if I come to understand the way I win here is by constantly losing? Then we might start to look like Jesus.

HOLY INDIFFERENCE

Number five is holy indifference in a world that always wants more. Those who have become part of the new humanity become relatively indifferent to their circumstances, primarily their material circumstances. "Indifference" means we get to the point where it really doesn't matter. Paul says it this way, "Sometimes I've had a lot, and sometimes I've had nothing, but in whatever circumstance, I've learned to be content because I can do all things through Christ who gives me strength." You notice that verse does have a context. The context of "I can do all things" is contentment, which means Paul thinks that's probably one of the hard ones.

And when we're talking about "I can do all things in Christ who gives me strength," we're usually talking about doing some incredibly difficult task. What Paul's talking about is the ability to be content when you have a lot of stuff and when you have nothing. Because it really doesn't make any difference to what's really important.

I like the words "holy indifference" because a lot of people who are committed to simple living seem so angry about it. It's not just that they want to simplify their lives. They want to simplify my life. And they're angry that they've made these sacrifices and I haven't yet. But it seems to me that once you've hit this point of holy indifference, you're like Jesus. You're able to walk into your rich family's home and enjoy the meal they serve you and the party they throw for you. And you'll be out there walking on the trail and have no place to lay your head and you're content there because it really doesn't make any difference. In a world that keeps demanding more and more, I wonder what would happen if we raised up a generation of people who were holy indifferent to such things? There are moments when I feel like we need to get really radical about this. I don't think we have much credibility with the world on this one. They've seen our homes and they've seen our buildings and we just really have nothing to say on this one. I wonder what would happen if we became indifferent.

Joy Beyond Circumstances

Number Six. We would be joyful in a world of dissatisfaction. One of my favorite definitions of Christianity: Jesus only promised his followers three things—they would be entirely fearless, absurdly happy, and always in trouble. This joy is not based on external circumstances; it's based on knowing who you are in God. We live in an American culture where creating dissatisfaction is a major industry. It's called advertising. A large part of the task of advertisers is to make you dissatisfied with what you currently have. They are way good at it. I mean they almost persuade me to buy things I have no use for. I almost bought aluminum siding. I've got a brick house. When I start buying things for the wife I know they are too good at what they're doing.

There's a really fine German philosopher named Arthur Schopenhauer, a contemporary of Kant. One of the reasons why Schopenhauer is not very well known today is because Kant was better. I know how he feels. I've spoken at conferences opposite Max Lucado. Max speaks in the main auditorium. I'm speaking in the broom closet to my immediate family who are all resentful to be missing Max.

And that was poor Schopenhauer. People would be streaming by his class to get to Kant's. But he was a pretty fair philosopher who wrote some really powerful things on desire. His says that desire is so treacherous because, when desire is fulfilled, what you immediately do is desire something else. Desire really is an insatiable monster. And if you try to defeat this monster by fulfilling desire you are really on the slippery slope, because you're never going to be finished with that one.

My experience is that's somewhat true. You know, you buy a computer and then, guess what, somebody built a faster one. And no matter what it is, there's always one that's better. Schopenhauer says somehow we've got to cut out this problem at the root. Now his solution was altogether implausible, but I do like the diagnosis of the problem. The problem with desire and dissatisfaction is once you get satisfied in a certain way then you have whole new ways of being dissatisfied.

And in the new humanity, we don't go there. Other than Jesus himself, the best theorist of the new humanity was Paul. When you hear Paul talk you can hear how he's got this joy that cannot be shaken by dissatisfaction. He'll say stuff like, "For me to die is gain." No threat there. "For me to live is Christ." Okay, no problem there. Or, if you want to take stuff from Paul, he says, "I count everything I've ever done or achieved as rubbish for the sake of Christ. You going to take stuff from me? You can't take anything from me. I don't have anything." So you think, "Okay, we'll buy you off." Paul's response is, "What are you going to give me? God has given me all things." He's got it. You can't create dissatisfaction in those who have nothing you can take from them and nothing you can bribe them with. You can't threaten them with death and you can't let them live. That's the new humanity.

GENUINE PRESENCE

The last one: the new humanity is marked by presence in a world of distraction. This is a complicated theological point in some ways. The outcome is simple enough. The place where God is most deeply and fully present is always here and now. He is a God of the past and he is a God of the future, but more than anything else, he is a God of the here and now. And as we experience God's presence in each moment, we live in the present. We do not live in the past. We do not live in the future. We live in the present moment where God is fully present. Some of you know people who live in the past. They can't let the past go. I deal with young people all the time who largely live in the future. They're constantly thinking about what they're going to do when. And my question is always the same: "What makes you think you'll be somebody different three years from now than you are right now?" Today is the day of God's presence. Now is the moment of salvation. So we pay attention to this moment with some confidence that God will be present in the next one.

James says, watch out for that person who says, "Tomorrow I'm going to go and do such and such." He says, "You don't know anything about tomorrow. You better pay attention to today, to this moment, because that's what you've got."

We live in a world where it is increasingly difficult to be present where we are. Just to annoy my students I tell them, "In my day we had a different word for multi-tasking. We called it being rude." I am weary to death trying to talk to somebody when they're doing three other things. And I'm irritated with myself when I'm like that. It's another thing that I really admire about Jesus. He seems to get things done, some things that need to get done, but he is so present where he is that he can have an encounter with a person that takes mere moments but in those moments it is as if Jesus and that person were the only people in the world. He's that present.

We have some theological prejudices built in here. We have a sacred and secular distinction in our minds. And I won't argue that there's nothing to that, but I would argue there's not much to it. Okay, what is sacred time? Sacred time is any time when God is present. Okay, what time would that be?

What is sacred place? Well it's anywhere God is present. Okay, now where would that be? I'm wondering if I'm out there dealing with people if perhaps I should be as present as I am in prayer. Because God is just as present in that sacred moment as he is in this one. And I wonder what would happen if we lived in a world like that. I don't think technology did that one to us. I think we were ready to go there, but it helped push us.

INVITING OTHERS INTO THE NEW HUMANITY

Here's what I'm offering. Peace and calm in a frantic world. A humble self awareness in a posturing world. Open nonjudgmentalism in a tribal world. Other regard in a narcissistic world. Joy in a world of dissatisfaction. Holy indifference in a world that wants more. Presence in a world of distraction.

What would it mean to take the risk of faith and adopt a new humanity that looks like Jesus, then inviting people to see if there's anything to this way of living? Because if what we're primarily offering them is simply some sort of intellectual choice about whether the world makes more sense with or without a God, or if what we are offering them is some sort of religion to add on to their already busy lives (that is, now you've got church on top of everything else), then it seems to me we're offering them the wrong stuff.

What we are offering them through Jesus is the new humanity in a world that's lost it. What we're offering is a new way of being in the world. Once a person takes Jesus seriously and comes and follows, they find that God comes and meets them there. When they take the risk of faith they find that God is faithful. Now that is a much messier way to do evangelism, to do church, to do gospel, but it seems to me it is very in tune with where the world is now.

Another way of saying it is this: If we're going to make a difference in the world, what the world primarily needs to see is a sustained Christian presence and witness in the world. And that is done not primarily by preaching in our churches, but by living out the values of the new humanity in a world gone wild where truth is no longer an assumption.

Chapter Nine

GOSPEL AFTER THE DEATH
OF TRUTH

T ruth is having a bit of a harder time that it once did. Back in the good
old days, we at least had this agreement that there was some truth. We
might have a disagreement about what that truth is, but there was no disagreement that there was a right or wrong to this and one of us is right and
one of us is wrong. And wasn't the world simpler then?

In a terrific paragraph in his huge book *Truth and Method,* Hans-Georg
Gadamer has this wonderful description of conversation. I won't quote it
exactly but I'll get really close. He said conversation is not me trying to persuade you to my point of view or you trying to persuade me to yours; it's
where we're both trying to be persuaded by this third thing which we call the
truth. It's this wonderful notion that our conversations are all about trying to
approach this thing that we call the truth. But in this day we would not only
have disagreements about what that truth is, there would be some disagreements about whether such a thing exists.

This leads in my students to sloppy relativism. "You have your opinion
and I have mine." Which is really strange when you think about it. So I am
concerned with how Christianity's truth claims function in a world where the
very notion of truth is somewhat under erasure. What I want to think about is

how we adjudicate truth claims within the Christian household. And I'm particularly concerned with how I evaluate my own experience and try to figure out if it's true or not.

Evaluating Experience

I was preaching at a church and a couple comes to me who are having trouble in their marriage. I'm to help them with this. That's an excellent description of just how desperate this situation was. And it turned out to be really quite fascinating. We're talking along and they're having these problems and just out of the blue she says, "God has spoken to me and told us we are not to have sex anymore."

Her husband's head whips around. I said, "Has God spoken to you on this?" And he says, "No."

What I thought was a really boring counseling thing is now theologically interesting. I'm wondering how this would work itself out. And so I say to her, "Well, this is interesting because I think God has already spoken to this one in 1 Corinthians 7."

I took them to the passage. It's interesting. They didn't quite know this one was there. The passage says that husbands and wives are not to withhold sex from one another except for a brief time to devote themselves to prayer and then come back together lest they be tempted. So we have this interesting theological problem now. Is she going to trust what God has said particularly to her or is she going to trust what God has said to the whole church. And then I sit back to see how it would come out. And I was really interested. I wasn't as interested as the husband was, but I was interested. It was more of a theological interest to me than to him.

And the wife says, "Well, I think I've got to trust what God's saying to me."

So there is a claim I'm not convinced by. And the problem is not just sorting out the claims of other people, but the more pressing problem of sorting out my own experiences. I have times when I wonder if that is the voice of God or is my superego working overtime here? Do we have God or psychology here? God or Freud? What a choice! And so I want to think a little about that.

Jesus claims that he is the way, the truth and the life. And so as a Christian, if I've got this right, Jesus is claiming to be the criterion for truth.

JESUS AS RESURRECTION TRUTH

Look at John 11. As you know, there are very few miracles in the book of John but there is a whole lot of talk about each one. And the talk is often as important as the miracle itself. So let's look at the conversation.

On his arrival Jesus found that Lazarus had already been in the tomb for four days. Bethany was less than two miles from Jerusalem and many Jews had come to Martha and Mary to comfort them in the loss of their brother. When Martha heard that Jesus was coming she went out to meet him, but Mary stayed at home.

"Lord," Martha said to Jesus, "if you had been here my brother would not have died, but I know that even now God will give you whatever you ask."

Jesus said to her, "Your brother will rise again."

Martha answered, "I know he will rise again in the resurrection at the last day." Jesus said to her, "I am the resurrection and the life. He who believes in me will live even though he dies and whoever lives and believes in me will never die. Do you believe this?"

"Yes Lord," she told him.   JOHN 11:17-27

Martha makes a profound confession, "I know he will rise again in the resurrection at the last day." But Jesus is not quite satisfied with that. I don't know if in the Pharisees-Sadducees debate she's saying "I'm with the Pharisees; I believe in the resurrection." So Jesus comes back with, "I am the resurrection and the life." This piece of theology about the resurrection on the last day is grounded in Jesus Christ himself. He is the truth of the resurrection.

JESUS, THE CENTER OF WORSHIP

In the previous chapter, I gave you a list, and there was something a little bit artificial about describing the new humanity from a list. The more accurate way to describe the new humanity is not to give a list but to point you to Jesus.

Let me show you another place where this happens in a different way. In John 4 Jesus is having this conversation with a Samaritan woman. "Sir," the woman said, "I can see that you are a prophet. Our fathers worshiped on this mountain but you Jews claim that the place where we must worship is in Jerusalem." Okay, she raises a sticky theological problem. Is the proper place of worship Jerusalem or Mt. Gerizim? That's a Jew-Samaritan split. Jesus declared, "Believe me woman, a time is coming when you will worship the Father neither on this mountain nor in Jerusalem. You Samaritans worship what you do not know. We worship what we do know for salvation is from the Jews. Yet a time is coming and has now come when the true worshipers will worship the Father in spirit and truth. For they are the worshipers the Father seeks. God is spirit, and his worshipers must worship in spirit and in truth."

So on this theological debate he says, "If I have to choose between Jerusalem or Gerizim, I'll take Jerusalem." The Jews have it right. The Samaritans have it wrong. But he says the question is quickly becoming passé. Why? Because the center of worship is no longer a place, it is a person. The center of Christian worship is standing right in front of her. And worship from this point forward will not be judged in the old ways, it will be judged by what it looks like in the light of Jesus.

SEEING THE TRUTH OF JESUS

In John 9 we have a story about Jesus healing a man born blind. Again you have the miracle and then you have lots of talk.

His neighbors and those who had formerly seen him begging asked, "Isn't this the same man who used to sit and beg?" Some claimed that he was.

Others said, "No, he only looks like him."

But he himself insisted, "I am the man."

"How then were your eyes opened?" they demanded.

He replied, "The man they call Jesus made some mud and put it on my eyes. He told me to go to Siloam and wash. So I went and washed, and then I could see."

"Where is this man?" they asked him.

"I don't know," he said.

They brought to the Pharisees the man who had been blind. Now the day on which Jesus had made the mud and opened the man's eyes was a Sabbath. Therefore the Pharisees also asked him how he had received his sight. "He put mud on my eyes," the man replied, "and I washed, and now I see."

Some of the Pharisees said, "This man is not from God, for he does not keep the Sabbath."

But others asked, "How can a sinner do such miraculous signs?" So they were divided.

Finally they turned again to the blind man, "What have you to say about him? It was your eyes he opened."

The man replied, "He is a prophet."

The Jews still did not believe that he had been blind and had received his sight until they sent for the man's parents. "Is this your son?" they asked. "Is this the one you say was born blind? How is it that now he can see?"

"We know he is our son," the parents answered, "and we know he was born blind. But how he can see now, or who opened his eyes, we don't know. Ask him. He is of age; he will speak for himself."

And then, verse 22, the critical verse in my estimation: "His parents said this because they were afraid of the Jews for already the Jews had decided that anyone who acknowledged that Jesus was the Christ would be put out of the synagogue. That was why his parents said he is of age, ask him."

Well, I won't take a long time to do this but I'm convinced John has written at a time when it has become clear that Christians are not just an odd sort of Jew. They are some other thing entirely. And so they are starting to get kicked out of the synagogues. And I think the Jews are jumping on them and saying, "What is it with this Jesus guy? He was killed as a common criminal." So John is writing his book to tell Christians that getting kicked out of the synagogue is no big deal because this guy wasn't a common criminal, he was the Son of God.

Now all this is important because when you come to John 20:30-31 he says he wrote the book "that you might believe." Now our assumption has always been that John is an evangelistic tract. But anybody who's ever really tried to use it that way knows that's highly unlikely. I mean if you're going to do evangelism it's a lot easier to do it out of Mark than it is John because you can skip the prologue.

I think John is writing that people will believe. And I think the people he's trying to get to believe are Christians. He's trying to get Christians to believe their confession that Jesus is Lord by trying to show them he's not this common criminal. He's this Son of God. Look again at how the parents look in this story. They look awful. They look like they're more concerned with their place in the synagogue than the healing of their son. So John is writing to these Christians who are trying to decide whether they're going to stick with this or not.

In contrast to the parents, John says,

> A second time they summon the man who had been blind. "Give glory to God," they said. "We know this man is a sinner." He replied, "Whether he is a sinner or not I don't know. One thing I do know. I was blind but now I see!" JOHN 9:24-25

I do want to point out that here is an appeal to an experience.

> Then they asked him, "What did he do to you? How did he open your eyes?" He answered, "I told you already and you did not listen. Why do you want to hear it again? Do you want become his disciples too?" JOHN 9:26-27

Good move. I like this guy.

Then they hurled insults at him and said, "You are this fellow's disciple! We are the disciples of Moses! We know that God spoke to Moses, but as for this fellow, we don't even know where he comes from."

The man answered, "Now that is remarkable! You don't know where he comes from yet he opened my eyes. We know that God does not listen to sinners. He listens to the godly man who does his will. Nobody has ever heard of opening the eyes to the man born blind. If this man were not from God he could do nothing."

To this they replied, "You were steeped in sin at birth. How dare you lecture us!" And they threw him out.   JOHN 9:28-34

This passage is trying to show these early Christians that they have hitched their wagon to the right guy, and that's Jesus. And all of this dust that's being thrown up by the Jews around them shouldn't obscure the notion that this is the guy who makes the blind see. He is the one who has resurrection power. He is the center of worship.

It seems to me a good deal of what John is doing is trying to get us to see things through the eyes of faith. And so in some places what you think you're seeing is not the whole story. What you think you're seeing is the death of the man Jesus but what you're really seeing is God glorifying his Son who, when he's lifted up, will draw all people unto him.

LOOKING BEYOND THE SUPERFICIAL

Sometimes you need to hear the message that following Jesus means dying, taking up the cross. Sometimes that's not the message you need to hear at all. Sometimes you are so beaten up by life and are feeling like such a loser that what you need to hear is that's not the whole story. Because Jesus is lifted up. He draws all people unto him. And he is as in control now as he was then. In John he doesn't even die. It says he gives up his spirit. Nobody kills him. Jesus is absolutely in control here and sometimes that's the message we need to hear.

John is trying to say, "You have to see things in a certain way. You have to see beyond the obvious to the transcendent." I think John, more than the other gospels, profoundly says it's not just about what you see; there are some spiritual realities that are taking place here behind this. Don't be superficial. Look deep and see the truth of this, which is God redeeming the world to himself through Jesus Christ.

I have been led to think again about the nature of evil by re-reading Hannah Arendt's book *Eichmann in Jerusalem*. You remember back in the 1960s, Eichmann was one of the last of the high ranking Nazis that hadn't been captured. Jewish secret police went down to South America, kidnapped him, brought him back to Jerusalem, held a show trial, and then hanged him.

Hannah Arendt went to report on this trial and then wrote a book about it. She says that we want Eichmann to be a monster, but the sad fact of the matter is he's not. In fact, he's pitiful. He is this bureaucrat whose major accomplishment was to make the trains run on time. He was given "the Jewish problem" and tried to solve it efficiently because he wanted to move up the ranks. She said he's not a monster, but a stunningly ordinary person. She describes this whole thing with this telling phrase: the "banality of evil." And her controversial conclusion finally is that evil is not something deep. In fact, evil is the failure to see anything deep. Evil is ultimately banal and superficial.

I don't know if she's right about that or not, but it's got me thinking that this philosophical and cultural climate we're in pressures toward seeing things superficially. I'm not using the word superficial lightly here. We see things on the surface. That's what Jesus came to change.

Look at 2 Corinthians 5:16: "So from now on we regard no one from a worldly point of view. Though we once regarded Christ in this way, we do so no longer. Therefore, if anyone is in Christ he is a new creation. The old is gone, the new has come." There's some weird epistemology going on here. Epistemology is about how you know stuff. And the conclusion is we no longer regard people from a worldly point of view though we once regarded Christ in this way. If I'm understanding this right, he's saying that now we see Christ in a different way and when we see Christ in a different way what happens is we see everything in a different way. This is the new creation.

And so seeing Christ from a worldly point of view means that at one point we saw Christ as this person who tried to get a religious movement going; he had some success, got into problems with the Jewish authorities, and got himself killed. End of story. We once saw Christ that way, but we don't any longer. And when we see Christ in another way—as God reconciling the world to himself—that means we see everything else in an entirely different way than we saw it before.

I would describe this as the experience of truth. The experience of truth is seeing the world through the story of Jesus Christ. And so we interpret our experience through the story of Jesus. We judge our interpretations of our experience by how they line up with the story of Jesus. Because that's the way we see the world now. And what we do is invite others to join us in seeing the world this way.

DOING THE TRUTH OF JESUS

I have taught ethics for years. By the time my students are done with my ethics class they generally can think in far more sophisticated ways than they could when they came in. This does not always mean they behave better. They would be able to give you a better explanation of why what they just did was wrong.

I teach a form of pluralistic deontology. That is, I think there are certain duties that you are bound to do regardless of the consequences. As opposed to utilitarianism, which would say you decide what you're going to do based on what you think the likely outcomes are. Does that make sense to you? There are some things you ought to do even if the consequences are going to be negative for you, so you don't do ethics on a cost benefit calculation; you do it based on these duties. I spell out to them what these duties are. But at the end of the day, what I have is what I would describe as an ethic of minimum civility. Or to put it another way, I teach them how to be a minimally decent Samaritan.

Now, that would lift the world's ethics a good deal. We are a long way from reaching the level of minimally decent ethics. One quick example. Philosophically the duty to do no harm is much stronger than the duty to do good. You believe that. Because you do not feel the obligation to do all of the good in the world you possibly could. Right? The example I give them is, if you're driving down the highway and you see somebody who has a flat tire, you may not feel the obligation to stop and help them, but the very least you could do is try not to swerve over there and pick them off. So it's do no harm and, if we can, let's do some good. Philosophically speaking, the obligation to do good is based on two things: the benefit to the other and the cost to ourselves. And they are related in this way. The lower the cost to myself and the higher the benefit to the other, the stronger the obligation I have. Sometimes the cost to myself is so low and the benefit to the other is so high that the obligation to do good is virtually as strong as the obligation to do no harm.

It's simple to illustrate. You remember when that plane out of Washington DC didn't get up high enough quickly enough, hit that bridge over the Potomac River, and went in? You remember the one guy who kept passing the rescue hook to other people, and eventually drowned in that icy water. Well, I asked my students to imagine that I'm standing on the bank of the Potomac that day and I see that plane go in. And I'm not a particularly good swimmer. I said, "Would I have an obligation to jump into that icy water and swim out there and try to rescue somebody?" Most of them agree that I'm not morally reprehensible for not doing that. It would be extremely heroic and laudable if I did, but I'm not doing something seriously immoral by not doing that.

Let me give you another case. Let's suppose I'm walking down the path by a little babbling brook and I discover that a little two year old toddler has stumbled in there. And you know how they are, they're like turtles. And he's fallen face first and he can't get up and he's flopping around and it's obvious he's drowning. And I can, by stepping into the water, grab him by the back of the shirt and pull him out. But if I do that, I'm going to get my incredibly attractive shoes wet. Now most of you would think that if I don't get my shoe wet to rescue that little fellow that I'm doing something seriously immoral, right? The cost to myself is very low and the benefit to the other is very high. This is what we would call an ethic of minimum civility. No problem.

Now, if you introduce Jesus into this, he really messes things up. You will see the world in a completely different way. If somebody is going to sue you and take away your coat—hey, just give them your cloak also. You have this Good Samaritan story. You have this story about "Go and sell all that you have and give it to the poor." What ethic is that? You know the church has been working for 2,000 years to explain away that command. If we start a redaction program in the Bible that's the place I want to start. Let's redact that one out. I don't want to go there.

How many times should I forgive the one who sins against me? Seven times? No—77 times. Have you lost your mind? What is this? Now we are seeing the world in a completely different way. He is calling you to an ethic that cannot be philosophically justified. It only makes sense when you accept the offer to "come follow me." One problem is that we ask people to accept the ethic of Jesus before they've accepted the call to come follow. That is not going to work. You first have to answer the call to come follow and then this ethic comes into play. Until then, I'm satisfied if I can get people up to an ethic of minimum civility.

One of the things I always want to know if I have a conflict with a student is whether this student claims to be a follower of Jesus Christ or not. Because the conversation goes in a completely different way if they are. If they're not, then I've got to talk to them about stuff like how much power I have in this situation, etc. But if they're a follower of Jesus Christ, then I can say, "Okay, let's think about how baptized people behave. What does one who takes seriously the call to come and follow Jesus do in a situation like this?" We see the world in a completely different way. And we come, in my opinion, to experience the truth that the surface is not all there is. There is this transcendent spiritual dimension because we no longer see Christ from a worldly point of view, and that means we don't see anything else from that point of view either.

I'm talking primarily about ethics at the moment because I think that is really on the front burner in our society. I want to know how one who takes seriously the call to come and follow Jesus sees issues like war and peace. I want to know how they see issues like wealth and poverty. I want to know how we see issues like over-commitment. I want to know how we see issues like family and materialism. Because we see them in a completely different way by virtue of answering the call to come and follow Jesus.

But this doesn't just apply to ethics. It applies to everything else too. For instance, if I'm trying to make sense of some experience and trying to figure out whether it's God or me, the first thing I'm going to do is read whatever that experience is over against my commitment to be a follower of Jesus Christ.

For example, I have almost no enemies because to really have an enemy you've got to have more personality than I do. I am just too bland to make much of an enemy. It's not that I haven't tried, but it just doesn't seem to take. Instead of making me their enemy they tend to just pat me on the head. But let's say that maybe someone writes something uncomplimentary about me that isn't true. I could work myself up into a lather and say, "You know, that person is always doing that to different people and I believe that God has called me to fix this problem." Let's see, how can we fix it? Well, let's hire a private detective. Maybe we can get pictures. That would solve this problem. Maybe I want to challenge them to a debate or I want to say ugly things. I mean, there are just all sorts of possibilities here and I can convince myself that God is calling me to do something to them. But before I act on that, I'd better come back and say, "How does this look if you take being a follower of Jesus seriously." Because then it might start to look completely different.

All of us who preach must feel some call to issue a prophetic message to our churches. There are times when our churches need to hear messages that they do not want to hear. But we are on treacherous ground then. We better run that through the ministry of Jesus in really serious ways before we say a word. Because we can talk ourselves into anything. And when you're called to come and follow Jesus you don't abuse people.

There's my case the best I can make it. What it means to have gospel after the so-called death of truth is to experience the truth that is found in Jesus Christ. And one of the things we do is accept the notion that we are not going to see things superficially. We may have seen them that way once, but now we see them through the lens of the life and ministry of Jesus Christ. And now we're not just looking at a list, we're looking at a life, and that life sorts out for us what gospel is. What would it be like to see the world through the lens of the confession that we believe Jesus is the truth? When you bring Jesus in, it gets interesting.

The Kingdoms of Earth and the Kingdom of God

Chapter Ten

GOD'S KINGDOM OVER ALL

My passion is to create conversation, in this case, peaceable conversations about the relationship of the church and the state. My concern is not for political scientists. If you're a professional political scientist, you won't read anything here that's the least bit interesting to you. I have no great expertise in political theory. I am not a Republican, a Democrat, or a Libertarian. I think I would most closely be identified as a cynic. I have deep roots in the political thought of David Lipscomb (that will mean something to some of you), but I am not going to be staking out political positions.

THE IMPORTANCE OF PERSPECTIVE

What I do hope to do is provide helpful perspectives on an important conversation. I'm more and more impressed with how important perspective is. Everybody has a story on this. Last summer I was trying to get home from Minnesota, which meant traveling through Dallas. The weather is terrible in Dallas, so we circle the Dallas-Ft. Worth airport a few times. Finally, we give up and fly to Tulsa, which is not even in Texas, is not on my itinerary, and has nothing to do with anything I'm interested in. We sit there for a couple of hours. The weather clears off in Dallas-Ft. Worth. We get in line to have our plane refueled. We get refueled and take off again and now we're on our way to Dallas. We land in Dallas. We were supposed to be there about 6:30. We're there at 10:30 and our gate is occupied. So we sit there another 45 minutes and finally get to the gate.

At this point I have abandoned all hope of getting to Abilene that late. They turn off the lights on our runway a bit earlier than that. But one plane is left going to Abilene. I make that flight. I'll be home around midnight and I think, "It's been a long day, but I've had worse." We start to land in Abilene, but the pilot takes the plane back up. He comes on the intercom and says, "Sorry, bad visibility. We're going to Dallas-Ft. Worth."

We arrive in Dallas-Ft. Worth at 1:00 A.M. They've had such a bad day in Dallas-Ft. Worth that all the hotels that they use to put up stranded travelers are full. We start to rebook our flights, and the earliest flight that they can book us on leaves at 5:30 that afternoon. They were remarkably unsympathetic, so I started looking around and I found three youngish looking people. I'd never seen any of them before. I walked up to them and I said, "Okay, here's the deal. I have got more money than I have energy. I will rent a car if you will drive it to Abilene." They said, "Let's do it." We rent us a car, and I ride to Abilene with three people I have never seen before.

I arrive home about 5:30 A.M. and sleep half an hour before work the next day. Isn't that the saddest story you've ever heard? I was able to generate a great deal of sympathy with that story for about two weeks. What happened two weeks later is hurricane Katrina hit, and all of a sudden my story didn't seem so sad, it just seemed amusing. I had my house. I had my bed. So I was inconvenienced for a few hours. I didn't have my life destroyed. Everything was brought into perspective.

I'm not very optimistic about changing your mind, but I'd like to create some perspective. I want to do three things. First, I want to tell you why the question about church and state is very important right now. Then I want to do some exegesis of a biblical text. Finally, I'll do some time thinking about how Christians can engage the culture and the political process.

CHURCH AND STATE TODAY

I made a pledge many years ago that I would never preach in a setting where there was an American flag in the sanctuary. I've preached in that situation now twice in a row for the last two weeks. I've probably done it a dozen times in the last two years. My absolute principles have collapsed under compromise after compromise. Those of you who know me well will not be surprised by this. But if you're an absolutist like I was, maybe you'll agree that at least two factors make the topic complicated.

The first one is easy. 9/11/01. Which changed this discussion fundamentally. All of a sudden a topic that had been sleeping for a good long time became important again. On the Sunday after those tragic events, flags were in the sanctuary, patriotic songs were being sung, and serious questions were being raised about the place of God in a world of conflict largely defined in religious terms. And that has made this a persistent discussion ever since. That's the first storm cloud.

The second one has been the continuing bifurcation of the country into red and blue states and the engagement of evangelicals in politics. Evangelicals managed to turn at least some of the elections into a referendum on Christian values. Those Christian values turned out to be two things: abortion and homosexual marriage. I have a problem when Christian values get reduced to things that happen only below the waist. Christian values are a little bigger than that.

What has been blowing behind this all the time is the whole issue of Constantinianism. Let me explain that term. Christianity was oppressed by the Roman government for three centuries. Then Constantine becomes the emperor. He makes Christianity a legal religion. He actually becomes kind of a Christian himself; he doesn't appear to me to be a very good Christian, but that's beside the point. So Christianity becomes coupled with the power structure of its day and it manages to maintain that power for a good bit of the next 1,700 years.

Well, that's changing a bit today. Christians maybe aren't quite the power brokers that they once were, but nonetheless, we have this conversation about how Christians should use political power in a free society that allows them to do so. Is it proper? Is it healthy? My concerns are two. One is that this conversation is being held in some places with fairly sharp language. And the other problem is there are some places where it's not being held at all. I'm a little bit more worried about that. That is, maybe this is a conversation we should be having.

I have a few assumptions here. First of all, it seems to me the Bible has no political theory; it's not a political textbook. I don't see any possibility of developing a political theory out of Scripture. Jesus doesn't appear to have a great interest in running for office or holding one. He does seem to be a bit of a pain to those who do.

While the Bible has no political theory, all of its implications are political. That is, everything the Bible teaches has deep implications for the *polis* (Greek for city). So we must read Scripture politically. I can't imagine that there is any other way to read it. Scripture has implications for how we live together and how we relate to the government and how we relate to the world. So I will not say, "Okay, we're not bringing politics into the Bible." You don't have to bring them in. They're right there. There are all sorts of implications.

The reason I think this conversation is so important now is that it's not politics that is at stake here, it is the gospel. There is a great battle in American life over the Christian story. There is deep disagreement about what the gospel is and what its implications are. So I think this is really important. The implications of the gospel itself are at stake here.

Five Ways to Engage Politics

I want to talk about five ways that Christians engage the political process. I'm not going to take any stand on these ways at all, at least for now. These are the ways that you can engage the process ranging from the least to most intrusive.

Number one is persuasion. That is, one of the ways that we can be involved in the political process is to persuade people that certain things are right, certain things are fair, and certain things are just. And as far as I know, no one is suggesting that Christians ought not to do that. Everybody agrees that persuasion is at least one thing that Christians can do that is legitimate in the political process. I do this all the time. I try to be persuasive to people about what I think are the values of the kingdom of heaven.

The second level of involvement we might call ordinary political action. And what we generally mean by this is something like voting. That is, not only can I try to be persuasive, but I can vote. I can try to put people in office who seem to hold the values that I hold. Most Christians agree that this is a fine thing to do. Not all do. David Lipscomb wasn't too big on the idea. I'm a little unsure of it myself, but many Christians feel this is a legitimate form of engagement.

Number three: extraordinary political action. That is, sometimes we want to get involved at a little deeper level than just voting; we want to get out and be an activist. This could take several forms. You might actually run for office. You might participate in some sort of political campaign. You might get out and distribute leaflets. You might walk in a protest. There are all sorts of ways to get involved. And that's where it starts to get fun.

Number four: Civil disobedience. Now this is the one my students can never get. They skip straight from number three to number five. Number five is terrorism. There are some Christians (very few, but a few) who would argue that the use of violence is justified if the cause is serious enough. These would be people who would blow up abortion clinics, for instance, or other forms of such terrorist activity.

What is there that stands between extraordinary political action and terrorism? Civil disobedience. Civil disobedience is very different from terrorism and it's also different from extraordinary political action. Extraordinary political action is still working within the system doing things that are lawful. Civil disobedience is stepping outside of the law, not trying to destroy the government, but to change some unjust law.

Civil disobedience is my favorite, especially when the disobedient ones are creative. One of my favorite stories of civil disobedience is about a group of people who live in a certain part of town where the airport is located and they've been made all sorts of promises about what time the planes would go and what routes they would follow. None of those promises have been kept. They are so frustrated; they're trying to get some help; but nobody in town is interested in their problem because they like the convenience of the airport and it's not in their neighborhood. Can you relate to this? So if you're in this situation, what you have to do is convince people that they have a stake in this. What they decide to do is study the flight patterns to figure out when the airport is busiest. They organize themselves; they get on the interstate and clog up all the lanes driving 15 miles an hour, backing up traffic everywhere and making people miss their planes. All of a sudden the city is interested in their problems.

Is that cool or what? I spent part of my education years in Syracuse, New York, which is the home of the Berrigan brothers, Daniel and Philip. Anybody know these names? They were anti-war activists in the 1960s; after that, their issue was nuclear proliferation. The question in Syracuse always was, "Are they in jail or are they out?" Because every once in a while they would go out to the military base and chain themselves to a bomb. I like that. That's a good form of civil disobedience. It's also one of the reasons why there are so few pacifists in the world. People don't like them and pacifists have very little they can do to defend themselves. You get the idea. Of course, there are really world-changing forms of civil disobedience. Look at Rosa Parks. Where would we be without people willing to step outside the law, not to destroy the government, but to call attention to injustice?

Okay, so here we go. We've got persuasion, ordinary political action, extraordinary political action, civil disobedience, and terrorism. Generally speaking, everybody agrees that persuasion is all right and most people agree that terrorism isn't. The debate is usually on the three in between. What is proper or improper for Christians to do? What I want to do is just let that sit right here for the moment and move to a text.

KINGDOM TRUMPS GOVERNMENT

In Matthew 22 we have this question about paying taxes to Caesar.

Then the Pharisees went out and laid plans to trap him in his words. They sent their disciples to him along with the Herodians. "Teacher," they said, "we know you are a man of integrity and that you teach the way of God in accordance with the truth. You aren't swayed by men, because you pay no attention to who they are. Tell us then, what is your opinion? Is it right to pay taxes to Caesar or not?"   MATTHEW 22:15-17

Now there is a bit of a knotty problem at this point. Jewish folks were all over the map in the opinion they took on this. The tax had to be paid in Roman money that declares that Caesar is some sort of God, so some saw it as unfaithfulness to God to pay taxes. On the one hand, if Jesus says, "Yes, you should pay taxes," they would say, "See, Jesus is more faithful to Caesar than he is to Torah." On the other hand, if he says they shouldn't pay taxes, then he's disloyal and causing insurrection because he's telling people they don't have to pay their taxes. They had him either way.

But Jesus, knowing their evil intent, said, "You hypocrites, why are you trying to trap me? Show me the coin used for paying the tax." They brought him a denarius, and he asked them, "Whose portrait is this? And whose inscription?"

"Caesar's," they replied.

Then he said to them, "Give to Caesar what is Caesar's, and to God what is God's."

When they heard this, they were amazed. So they left him and went away.   MATTHEW 22:18-22

It does not say whether he returned the coin. Now this answer is not just clever, although it is that. There is some real theological baggage in the answer and I want to tell you what I think three of those things are. The way he answers the question suggests, first of all, that Jesus recognizes the legitimate sphere of government. There is a realm that is properly Caesar's. Jesus is not an anarchist. He's not anti-government. He believes government has a role—he's not trying to do away with government. He's not suggesting that somehow the spiritual kingdom of God makes government irrelevant or unnecessary. He's not doing anything like that. Government has a legitimate sphere.

Second, he further suggests that when government is occupying its legitimate sphere the proper response by his followers is obedience. He doesn't say you've got to figure out what this tax money is going for. Some might say if part of your tax money is going toward persecution of Christians, then you need to figure out what that percentage is and deduct that amount before you pay your taxes. He doesn't do anything like that. He is straightforward; when the government is doing what the government is supposed to be doing, your proper response is to be obedient. Now this is a little bit minimalist. He doesn't suggest anything more than simple obedience. He doesn't go so far as to say you ought to be patriotic. But he does say you ought to be obedient.

Third, the most important thing he does in this passage is to point out the relative nature of our commitment to government. How far does commitment to government extend? Exactly to that point where commitment to God requires something else. And if you look carefully through what Jesus teaches, this is a fairly consistent point in his teaching. We have all sorts of obligations in our lives. Our obligation to government is just one. Those are real and legitimate obligations, but they are relative to one's obligation to the kingdom of God. There is only one absolute obligation and that's it. Or to put it another way, the kingdom of God trumps everything. Now to try to get you to agree with this, let's look at other obligations

KINGDOM TRUMPS THE FAMILY

I think one of the really interesting things is Jesus' position on obligation to family. As far as I can tell, Jesus thinks you have legitimate and important obligations to family. He gives some who are not taking care of their aged parents a really hard time because they're saying everything they have is devoted to God. You've got these aging parents. They've become a nuisance and they simply will not die. And they are sucking up the resources as you try to take care of them and so what you do (because you're a deeply spiritual person) is say, "Mom and Dad, I'd like to keep helping you, but I can't because I have devoted everything I have to God. To give part of it to you would be stealing from God. I know you wouldn't want me to do that, so good luck."

Jesus condemns that. You've got obligations to your parents. Obligations to children. But the kingdom of God even trumps family. Sometimes in order to pursue the kingdom of God, you must hate father and mother. You must refuse to obey the king. And sometimes you've got to let the dead bury their dead. I've said before that we often get these kind of questions misplaced. As far as I can tell from Jesus' teaching on the afterlife, family doesn't seem to be functioning in the afterlife. In other words, the relationships we have in family are important but temporary. The relationships we have in the kingdom of God are eternal and thus primary.

I think that's one of the important things in Jesus' conversation with the rich young ruler. You remember the funny way that winds up. The unfunny part is the rich young ruler goes away sorrowful and then the disciples say, "Hey, we've given up everything to follow you; how about us?" And Jesus says everybody who has done that will receive all this stuff and then he goes into this "fathers and mothers and sisters and brothers." I'm thinking, "Wow, that's strange. How do I get that? Do I want that? When I think about my own family I think, do I want more of that?" I think what he's offering there is the church. He says whatever relationships you lose in pursuing the kingdom of God you find again inside the kingdom. Most of you have become family to someone who is not your blood because of your relationship in the kingdom of God. For that other person that relationship has become more important than blood. And so these commitments to family are important but they're relative—the ultimate commitment is to the kingdom of God. One of the things I always say when I go into churches is this: If you're still asking the question, "What is this church doing for families," you better start asking the other question, too, "How are these families serving the kingdom of God?" Because the kingdom doesn't exist to serve families. Families exist to serve the kingdom. It is the kingdom that is absolute.

Now what is true of family is also true of government. Jesus recognizes that we have legitimate responsibilities to government, to be obedient to it in its proper sphere, but our responsibilities to that government are always relative to our responsibility to the kingdom of God. The kingdom of God trumps everything.

Kingdom Trumps Your Job

Now I'd like to see how many ways I can say that until I find the way that annoys you more. That's really tough. The kingdom of God trumps our responsibilities in vocation or job. I have this conversation with the students I teach all the time. It is highly likely, no matter what profession you choose, that somewhere down the line the demands of your profession and the demands of the kingdom will come in conflict. It is almost unimaginable that that won't happen. And it's precisely at that point that you find out your primary identification. I guess the one profession where that could never happen is preaching. I mean it's unimaginable that one's responsibility to one's particular church could ever come in conflict with one's responsibility to the kingdom of God, right? That's unimaginable.

I remember when I was at one church I had this one wonderful elder. He was an irritant. You know one of the things you find out in churches that have large elderships is that they assume certain roles. This guy's role was to be the irritant and he was gifted in that role. We're having this conversation about a difficult issue in our church and (as sensitive elders would) they're having a lot of discussion about if we do "x," how will our people react to it. But bless his heart, I love him to death, the irritant would always interject into those conversations, "Before we ask how people are going to react to this, let us ask what God would have us do. If the will of God is calling us some place contrary to what our people want to do, let's get out there." I don't know if I'd want him for my only elder, but I'd want one like him. Wouldn't you? It's possible even in a religious profession to get confused about what's primary.

I think about how many ways I can get my students to think about this. I ask my marketing students, "You're preparing yourself to sell people things they do not need. What are the limits of that? What are the limits that your commitment to the kingdom of God places on you professionally? Because if you don't think there are any, you haven't thought about this enough." There are some things you can't do because it brings you into conflict with the values of the kingdom of God.

Or with my journalism students. They're always interesting ones because they're always after the truth. They have no interest in the boring truth, only the interesting truth. And they're quick to say what their profession serves is truth. And I said, "Not if you're a Christian. We don't serve an abstract concept called truth. We serve the kingdom of God as expressed in Jesus Christ. That's not the same thing."

The question you have to ask all along the way is, "What are the limits that are placed on me professionally by virtue of the fact that my primary allegiance is to the kingdom of Jesus Christ?" You've been there. You've done that. You've seen that. Most of us have made our decisions imperfectly. Some of us have done it really badly. But at least we express our commitment that the kingdom of God trumps everything.

KINGDOM TRUMPS ALL

Okay, let me see if I can think of another provocative way or two to say it. I have more in common with an Iranian Christian I have never met who has sold out to the cause of Jesus Christ like I have than I do with my pagan next door neighbor who may share my political views. Because the kingdom of God trumps everything. We have this ceremony the first of the year at ACU where we march in all the flags of all of the countries where our students are from and then we march in the flags of all the states where they're from. None of us know what the Rhode Island flag looks like. We hope to find out one day. So we march them all in and we all cheer for our state or country flag. You know the Texas flag gets a big cheer because it's Texas, the state that was once a country and has never really gotten over that.

What I've suggested is to march in all those flags, march in the American flag too, march them all in, and have this big cross at the end of the room, and as you bring in every flag to the cross, dip it to the cross and then set it down. I got a feeling some people wouldn't be able to deal with that; but the kingdom of God trumps everything. That's who we claim to be.

It doesn't mean that the government has no legitimate sphere. It doesn't mean Christians don't have an obligation to be obedient to government. It just means there can be places where the commitment to government and the commitment to the kingdom can come into conflict and when they do this is what we say, "The kingdom of God trumps everything."

Now I hope you can at least partially see why I am saying I believe the gospel itself is at stake. That the kingdom of God trumps everything is very close to the heart of the gospel. This is what the gospel message is. We have been called into an allegiance that make all previous allegiances relative. There are different ways to describe that. Let me tell you my favorite way. It's called being a Christian.

Now the notion of being a Christian has become so dumbed down that we have failed to appreciate the weight of it. When I say I'm a Christian, I am saying a lot. I am saying I have been called into a new reality that puts all of these other realities in a different perspective. It doesn't mean I was an American and I'm no longer an American. It just puts Americanism in a new reality because American is not my primary identifier. I'm an American Christian and "Christian" primarily identifies me. It's not saying I'm no longer single, but now I'm a single *Christian* which is the primary identifier. And it doesn't magically change my economic status. Its not that I'm no longer rich. I am. I finally have come to admit it. I am extravagantly wealthy. If you compare my wealth to the world as it is now, I'm way up there. I'm running out of things to compare myself to in order to stay poor. But "rich" is not my primary identifier. I'm a rich *Christian*.

So everything stays the same but everything changes. Now everything has been put in this relative position. Now I haven't yet said anything about what this does to our approach to ordinary political action, extraordinary political action, civil disobedience, and other ways that Christians can be engaged in the political process; nor have I talked about this vexing problem of nationalism and what we do about it. I'll do those next.

But I do want to end with a word of caution. One of my students is married to a military guy. They have a new baby named Jacob Israel. Curious name. Redundant, but I like it. It has everything. Jacob Israel. I like it. And her husband is shipping out to Iraq on Monday.

If she were reading this, what I would want her to hear is, "Boy, I know you're praying for him every day and I am too." My prayer for him, for his safety and well being, has got nothing to do with my understanding of the righteousness or unrighteousness of that conflict. It is my commitment to a brother and sister in Christ that I feel very deeply. I have great qualms about the use of power by Christians. But it is important that you not jump to the conclusion that those opposed to certain political actions are disloyal, disobedient, or bad Americans. Or to say it another way, on this issue as all others, how about we give each other the benefit of the doubt and create an atmosphere where we can have peaceable conversations about what we understand the gospel is and what it requires.

Chapter Eleven

POWER OR POWERLESSNESS?

I want to give two contrasting visions of Christian engagement in the nation. One I'm going to call "the ministry of power" and the other I'm going to call "powerlessness." The ministry of power says that Christians should get and use power, but they should do it only in certain ways and for certain causes. That's why it's the ministry of power. The other vision is that Christians don't have any business doing that at all, that in fact we are the people that have forsaken power because we worship a God who has made himself known in the cross. I want to lay out those competing visions in a way that you don't know which side represents my view.

A few years ago my friend Rubel Shelly was getting ready to debate an atheist in Iowa. What an atheist was doing in Iowa I have no idea, but anyway, I did a mock debate with him to help him prepare. Afterwards someone who heard both the mock and the real debates said I argued the atheist's point of view better than the atheist did. I said, "Now there's something to put on your resumé, isn't it?" But I do want to try to present both sides of this question persuasively.

Let me tell you about perhaps the most brilliant student I've ever had. He's the kind of guy who would listen to your lecture, not have any comments, and come back the next day having seen every problem and hole in it. He also developed a deep social concern. So he decided at one point that he was going to go to the Dominican Republic and pick tomatoes with poorly paid tomato pickers there. He was going to engage in solidarity with the poor. This didn't seem to me what he ought to do. I said, "Okay look, if you are really concerned about the poor, go to Harvard Law School, get yourself some power, and let's see what you can do with it." He sat there for a while and thought about it. He came back the next day and said, "The only problem with that is this. If I do that I may become what I have looked at and despised." So, those are two very different visions, right? One where I get some power to do something good, and the other where I forsake power entirely and throw my lot in with these people. Which one is right?

Using Power for Peace

First of all, let me talk about the ministry of power. I begin here with the assumption that if we seek power as Christians it would never, ever occur to us to use that power for our own sakes or for the sake of the powerful. In the Old Testament those who are given power have it as a ministry to be used in behalf of those who don't have any—the orphan, the widow, the stranger in the land, and the poor. To use your power to abuse those groups is really high crime.

I start out with this notion that if you believe the proper Christian engagement with society is the ministry of power then what we're talking about is using that power in behalf of those who don't have any. I would assume that it is also to attempt to instantiate the values of the kingdom of God in this society. And this is where I think we get into some confusion. What are the values of the kingdom? What do we try to use power for?

Number one, we use power to establish *shalom*, peace. We practice politics to exert the power of generating peace. We have experience with both kinds of people who have power: those who use their power to keep things constantly stirred up, and those who use power in behalf of *shalom*, well being for all. We should use our power to try to create this sense of well being.

I'm not a person who has any political power. I mean I don't have any power in my university. I tell people when I see them, "If you are not my boss at ACU, your career has really stalled, because I am so far down the pecking order." However, I do have a good bit of power. Now I'm not just talking about influence here. That's a different matter. I'm incredibly influential. I'm not talking about influence. I'm talking about power.

In my classroom with my students, I have enormous power. I have an almost divine power. The first day students come into my class as freshman I always give them these options. I say, "There are some things I will answer to and some things I will not. I do not answer to Dr. Harris. I do not answer to Mr. Harris. I certainly do not answer to Brother Harris. I will answer to Randy." And just to see if they know their Bible I say, "I also will answer to 'the power that is called great.'" Every once in a while walking across campus, I'll hear some kid yelling, "Oh, great power, Oh, great power," and I know that's me. I was standing with the university president once and some kid comes by and says, "Oh, great power." And I said, "He's not talking to you."

Now having this power is very seducing. When a student walks into my office, before I've ever said a word or met them, they're often intimidated. Now the question is this, "Do I want to play that power card or do I want to be hospitable? Do I want to be a welcoming presence? Do I want to create *shalom* for them?" That's just my little world. You project that on the big world and get some power. We're engaged. What are we going to do with it? Let's try to create some *shalom*.

USING POWER FOR JUSTICE AND INCLUSIVITY

The second value won't surprise you. Justice. If the Old Testament is to be believed, justice is very close to God's heart. It even says God is more invested in justice than he is in proper worship. In Amos God says, "I'm tired of your prayers and your songs, take them away. I wish you would just stop it. What I want is this, for justice to roll down like a mighty river."

It is unfortunate that when we think about the use of power in the Christian sense, we're usually not thinking about creating greater justice. Maybe we are, but it doesn't seem like it. Whenever we start using examples about how we need to use our Christian power in society we usually do not talk about justice issues. But justice in our society, I would argue, is the big issue. Now I don't have the solutions to all of our problems of injustice, but with whatever power I have I would want to create some justice.

The third value of the kingdom that we want to inculcate is inclusivity. I've been reading the gospels again because it seemed like I needed to. I teach "Life and Teachings of Christ" every fall and I am reading Luke, which has never been my favorite gospel. I like Mark. It's short. For my short attention span. Mark gets to the point and makes it brilliantly. Matthew has the Sermon on the Mount. And I don't know what John is doing. So I'm reading through Luke again. One of the ways of interpreting Luke is to see Jesus asking the question, "Who is invited to the party?" Because the religious leaders of Jesus' day have a very limited guest list. They were irritated about Jesus because he just keeps bringing in the riffraff.

In Luke 14 you have this famous parable of Jesus where this guy throws a great banquet and he invites these people but they all have some reason not to come. You remember this parable. What do we call it—the parable of the excuses? Listen to the reasons they can't come. The first said, "I've just bought a field and I must go and see it, please excuse me. Because if I don't go see that field it might get away." Another said, "I've just bought five yoke of oxen and I'm on my way to try them out. Please excuse me." Still another said, "I just got married, so I can't come." That's the only one that makes sense to me so far.

Boy, I love these parables of Jesus. Have you noticed how edgy they are? Great teacher, that Jesus. The servant came back and reported this to the master and then the owner of the house became angry and ordered the servant to go out quickly into the streets and alleys of the town and bring in the poor, the crippled, the blind and the lame. "Sir," the servant said, "what you ordered has been done but there is still room." Then the master told his servant, "Go out to the roads and country lanes and make them come in so that my house will be full; I tell you not one of those who have been invited will get a taste of my banquet." That's an edgy parable.

One of the values of the kingdom is inclusivity. If I have some power, one of the values I want to practice is inclusivity. I want to create a place at the table for everybody. One of the things that we found out after the Soviet Union fell apart is that it was only raw power holding that empire together and as soon as you took that power away tribalism broke out in the Balkans. We've seen this over and over again in Africa. We're seeing it in the news every night in Iraq. And I must tell you, just under the surface of American life there's just a whole bunch of tribalism. We're in tribes and it seems to me that what you would want to do if you had power is to create—not by sheer force but by the creative use of power—an inclusive world where everybody feels pulled up to the table and where some of those divisions would start to break down.

USING POWER TO GIVE DIGNITY

Number four is dignity. One of the things we do with power is work towards the dignity of all persons. I root this in my reading of the creation account where human beings are created in the image and likeness of God. And that gives them dignity. Because of that created nature they always deserve to be treated with a certain respect.

Now there are two different kinds of respect. And they're both fine things. The more common kind of respect is the respect we give people because of something they have achieved. We respect people because of their athletic accomplishments, their academic accomplishments, and their artistic accomplishments. We admire and respect them for what they can do. But there's another kind of respect, not so common, that we give to every person before they ever do anything or despite whatever they've done, simply because they're created in the image and likeness of God. And they're always worthy of that respect.

In one church where I was a member, every time our young people would accomplish something we would try to make a big deal of it. And you know I feel good about that. But the more I thought about it, the more it started not to hit me quite right. And so I would say to them, "We are really proud of what you've accomplished here and it doesn't matter to us at all. Because we won't love and respect you one whit less if you never finish in first. That's not where your worth lies. It lies somewhere else. We want you to know that we respect you for being created in the image and likeness of God. We don't have to have any other reason than that to respect you."

Power is so often used to destroy the dignity of people. If you've ever been in the position of being helped, you understand this. I had my starving graduate school years like a lot of people did. I didn't have it near as rough as some, but you know there was a time when I didn't have any money in my pocket at all. I'm going to one of the members of the church there to get a haircut and I don't have any money to pay him. I tell him, "I can't pay you until the first of the month." He says, "No problem." I get home and I've got this twenty dollar bill in my pocket. There are a lot of ways to give, but he did it so gently that it didn't dent my dignity at all. I spent the money.

We've probably all been in situations in our churches where we've done some benevolence and by the time we were done we had given some food away but we dented some dignity while we did it. I'm a lot better at helping people than I am being helped. I do mentoring groups and I'm always praying over students. Then they will ask, "What can we pray about for you?" and I'll say, "You don't have to pray for me, I'm the pray-er." But I am learning that I need their prayers. When they can pray for me it makes it a little easier when I need to pray for them. Sometimes I have a group that wants to take me out to dinner at the end of the year. They don't have the money and I do, so I want to pay for dinner. But I've learned to just say, "Thank you," because when the time comes and they need some help, if they've been able to help me it's a little easier to be helped in return. Dignity is a fundamental value of the kingdom.

USING POWER FOR ICONOCLASM

I'll focus on number five for just a moment. Iconoclasm. Now here's the definition: kill the holy cow. It's not a technical definition but that's what it means. What I mean is this. It is one of the values of the kingdom never to allow the kingdom to be equated with any other kingdom of the world. Whatever that other kingdom is, whether it is nation or church, when we point to it we say that is not the kingdom of God. It's the prophetic stance that we must always take to power. And one of the things we keep talking about is the gap between the call of the kingdom of God and life as we experience it now.

It is dangerous business not to take that prophetic stance. Christianity is so easily seduced, so easily taken captive by the powers of this world, that if we are going to enter into the power game as Christians we had better make sure we understand that what we're working for is temporary and partial. That it is not the kingdom of God.

Shalom, justice, inclusivity, dignity, compassion, iconoclasm. It is the ministry of power. If I were going to use power, these are the values of the kingdom that I would work for. This is the ministry of power.

No Forced Discipleship

Now let me say one more thing about that, and then I want to argue the other side. I said earlier that we don't use power for the sake of the powerful or in our own behalf. I want to talk about one other way we don't use power. We do not use power to compel acts of discipleship. That's not who we are. That's not what we do. If people are going to become disciples of Jesus, it is because they are going to answer the call of Jesus to come follow. To try to make people live out the ethic of Jesus before they become a disciple of Jesus is hopeless. It's like the old saying, this is like trying to teach a pig to sing. It is frustrating to both you and the pig.

The most that we can hope for out of the law or power is to call people to be, not good Samaritans, but minimally decent ones. I'm not too keen on Good Samaritan laws. I do think the law must require us to be minimally decent. But when we want to go beyond that and use power to try to compel people to be disciples, not only do I think that doesn't work, I think it's deeply perverse. That's not the way we do evangelism. Evangelism is an invitation to come and follow. It's an invitation to take up the cross. There's a logic of following Jesus that leads to all sorts of acts of discipleship. But to try to use our power to compel people into acts of discipleship who aren't disciples is a really bad idea.

Let me come at it another way. I don't want to use power in any way that I wouldn't be willing for it to be used on me. That is, I don't want to do anything with power I wouldn't be willing for somebody else to do if they had the power. Now this is increasingly important because nobody knows how the demographics of a country are going to change. On Sunday, 17.8 % of the population will be in church. Okay, can you do the quick math? How many does that mean won't be? 82% rounding it off. The number of people who are regular churchgoers is 24%, that means three out of four aren't. In the year 2050 there will probably be fewer than 12% of people in church regularly. If you listen carefully, what you hear is power shifting and it's not coming our way.

I'm not willing to use power to do something I wouldn't want others to do to me. That's why I'm not a big advocate of some sort of formalized prayer in schools. Because most of you would be greatly offended if a district was primarily Muslim and they did Muslim prayer in schools. You'd throw a fit. But some are willing to use power in ways that we wouldn't be willing for people to do to us. And you know Christians don't need permission to pray in school. What are we doing trying to make other people do it? Does that make sense to you?

I know my students pray. I have seen it in their eyes. I know they're praying when I'm not. Test days they pray. I seldom have a formalized prayer at the beginning of class on test days because I don't want to interrupt their praying. I do pray on days we're not having a test because they're not as prayerful on those days and they may need a little boost. Every once in a while I kind of help them. God and I have come to an agreement on this that it is okay. We have a little fun with them every once in a while. Like I'll be praying and it's a day we're not having a test and I'll say, "God, help these students on this test today." It is amazing. We have people text messaging during prayer.

Let me say it another way. I would neither a persecutor or persecuted be. I don't want to use power in ways that are persecutorial. I don't particularly want to be on the receiving end of that either. So I think we ought to be pretty restrained in our use of power to compel acts of discipleship. Which is very different than trying to use power in a way that creates *shalom,* justice, inclusivity, dignity, compassion, and iconoclasm.

POWERLESS FOR GOOD

Now let me say a few words about the second approach, the powerlessness approach that says the use of political power even in good causes is somehow inconsistent with who we are as Christians. Usually this is rooted in a deep commitment to an understanding of the cross. It is striking that God's most definitive act in the world is not an act of power but an act of powerlessness.

Back to the Gospel of John now. The reason I've always had trouble with John is it's very hard to find the human Jesus there. John is really preoccupied with showing us that Jesus is divine. What John makes clear is that Jesus in his divine power can at any moment take control and make happen whatever he wants to.

So he's in the garden and they come to arrest him. The soldiers ask, "Is Jesus here?" He says, "I am," and they all fall down. It's a sign that they can't even arrest Jesus unless he's ready for them to. They take him to Pilate who claims to have power. Jesus says whatever power Pilate has comes from God. And then Jesus goes to the cross and you have some really strange language. You've got all this agony on the cross in the synoptics, but in John, Jesus is doing a counseling session, making sure someone cares for his mother. Even the language of his death is striking. It doesn't ever quite say in John that he dies. He "gives up his spirit." That is, the only person who decides when Jesus dies in John's story is Jesus.

It is all about the power of Jesus, which makes it all the more striking when he decides to use none of it. And that's our story. All of a sudden I find myself with incredible power. What does it mean to call Jesus Christ Lord and Master when he has all this power but is not willing to use it? Instead, he lays down his life. Now we're talking about a different kind of politics. The politics that sets out from the beginning to lose. We usually don't go at it this way. We are not trying to get power, we're forsaking power. We're going to keep laying down our lives, even let others kill us, because God will raise us up. Our approach to the world is going to be simply laying down our lives over and over again. We are not going to use power.

My favorite passage on this theme is the obscure passage at the end of Hebrews that has everything I like in a passage. It has deep theology and it's just obscure enough where you might say you disagree with my view, but you really can't say I'm wrong.

> The high priest carries the blood of animals into the Most Holy Place as a sin offering, but the bodies are burned outside the camp. And so Jesus also suffered outside the city gate to make the people holy through his own blood. Let us, then, go to him outside the camp, bearing the disgrace he bore. For here we do not have an enduring city, but we are looking for the city that is to come.   HEBREWS 13:11-14

The city depicted here is Jerusalem. The problem Hebrews addresses is Christians slipping back into or considering returning to Judaism. Hebrews says that's all wrong. You don't try to return to the security of the city because Jesus is found outside the camp. So you go out to the place of insecurity and rejection and shame because that's where you find Jesus.

Let me make a comparison. We often think that the barbarians are at the gates. I can give you a long litany of evidence that the barbarians are at the gates, but you don't need that evidence. You read the newspapers, too. And when the barbarians are at the gates, what you do is you get up on the walls of the city and you protect the city because the barbarians are charging the city.

What's wrong with that? It's their city. We probably shouldn't have been in there in the first place. The problem is they belong in here and we belong out there. Bring them in and out we go where we belong, on the margins, outside with the tomato pickers, bearing the disgrace he bore. These are the Christians who will not fight. They're not cowards, because I assure you they are going to die. They're not going to fight because the one they call Lord and Master lays down his life. So these people don't enter into the traditional power competition that takes place in the political sphere. They stand outside of that. But it's not like they're unengaged. They lay down their lives for the poor. They lay down their lives for the dignity of other human beings. They lay down their lives to create *shalom*. They lay down their lives for the sake of justice and inclusivity. What they do not do is use power or fight. It's the ministry of powerlessness.

POWER OR POWERLESSNESS?

How did I do for even-handed presentations? In my ethics class the first thing I do is teach them a lot of ethical theory. And then the last few weeks of the course I take up some issues and divide the class into different teams to debate the issues. They don't get to pick which team they're on, so they often wind up arguing a position they don't believe. That's good for you, by the way. You don't know if you understand the position until you try to argue the side you don't believe.

One of the issues we're doing right now is the Christian and warfare. The groups debating it were taking the pacifist position or the just war position. One group takes the position of powerlessness for Christians. You could be engaged in all sorts of ways, but you don't use power. You don't fight. The other group is saying you don't fight over just anything, but there are some times when the stakes are so high and the issues are so horrendous that the only thing the children of light can do is take up arms against the children of darkness (to use Reinhold Niebuhr's words).

And my just war group said there's never been such a thing as a just war, but we think if there is a just war, fighting would be justified. And so I used one of the approaches to teaching I find very effective—humiliation. I said, "Please don't tell me that you have been preparing for weeks to present a position that you don't think has any real world application at all." They said, "We're not doing that." I asked them to give me an example of a just war. I was ready for World War II, because that's the one we usually go to. They said, "What we think would be a just war is one we're not in yet." I said, "Good grief, you're not going to try to justify one we've got; you're going to try to start one? Okay. Hit me with it."

This tells you something about the quality of some of our students' hearts. I keep being impressed. They said Darfur. Darfur is in the Sudan. There is a genocide going on there that I suppose is somewhat equal to what happened in Rwanda while we sat and fiddled. And they said we know it's going on, everybody knows it's going on, it's a dreadful thing, and we have the power. Then they decided to humiliate me. They said this is like standing on the side of the road seeing some huge guy beat a little old lady to death while you sit there and watch. They said, "What is it with Christians that just because a nation has no strategic importance they think those people don't count."

Now the issue is engaged. I say to my other side, my pacifist side, "Okay, you ungodly people, what do you have to say to that?" In teaching ethics, it's very important to be able to turn on a dime and switch sides. They said, "You're assuming that our position is because we don't think we should fight that we think we should do nothing. What would happen if hundreds of thousands of white Christians go over to that African nation and lie down and say, 'If you're going to kill them then you have to kill us first.'"

And there the issue is engaged. Should we use the ministry of power or a profession of powerlessness to engage and change the world?

Chapter Twelve

AMERICA OR CHRISTIANITY?

There is one line from *The Godfather* that has become extremely famous. It was famous in the book that Mario Puzo wrote years before and it became the defining line of the movie. The Godfather is trying to get somebody to do something he's not likely to want to do and so he says, "I'm going to make him an offer he can't refuse." Of course, I'm a postmodernist. You know what a postmodern Godfather does? He makes you an offer you can't understand.

I use *The Godfather* when I teach ethics because it's an extremely interesting case. What is the primary virtue in mafia ethics? Loyalty to the family. That becomes the value that trumps everything else. Now is loyalty a virtue or not? Well, loyalty looks really good if you're loyal to the right stuff, but if you're loyal to the wrong stuff I'm not so sure about it.

You probably see where I'm going. What if I change the word loyalty to a subset of loyalty called patriotism. Patriotism is basically a subset of the virtue of loyalty. Instead of loyalty to the family, patriotism is loyalty to country. Is it a virtue? Well, it looks pretty good when we're talking about loyalty to my country. When it's loyalty to somebody else's country, I get a little iffy about that. If patriotism is always a virtue then the terrorists who do what they do in the name of country are as patriotic as the person protecting people from terrorist acts, because both are being deeply loyal to their country. So patriotism or loyalty surely is a commendable aspect of our lives. It's a virtue.

But we probably don't want it to be *the* virtue. We probably don't want it to be the unconditional commitment of our lives or we could become the American mafia.

There must be something that moderates patriotism. Is loyalty to family a commendable virtue? I think most of you would say yes. Is loyalty to friends a commendable virtue? Most of you would say yes. Once in a while I like to try to test my students to find out where their loyalties lie. Let's see if you can do this one. What is the primary ethic of everybody in school from kindergarten up through college? "Thou shalt not rat on another student." Cheating is okay. Ratting on another student—never. Never. We must teach them to quit being so loyal to their friends. I don't want that loyalty to be the only player in the game. I don't want it to be the only virtue.

The Problem with Nationalism

So loyalty to country, loyalty to family, loyalty to friends—all of those strike me as commendable things. The problem is when patriotism becomes nationalism. Now this is a different matter. Nationalism is always evil because it is idolatry. It is the point where we confuse the nation with God, where our primary loyalties become aimed at the nation instead of God. This is always bad news. And nationalism is often lurking just under the surface of much of what we do.

There are a couple of different kinds of nationalism and most of us aren't guilty of the obvious one. We don't substitute the nation for God. We don't pray to the nation. We don't worship the nation. If you ask us, "Is the nation the most important thing in your life?" like good Christians we'd say, "Well, of course it's not. Jesus Christ is. The kingdom of God is."

We're not guilty of that crass kind of idolatry. I would say we're guiltier of a more subtle form. The best place for me to illustrate this is Exodus 32, the golden calf story. Not one of the Israelites' better moments.

> When the people saw that Moses was so long in coming down from
> the mountain, they gathered around Aaron and said, "Come, make

us gods who will go before us. As for this fellow Moses who brought us up out of Egypt, we don't know what has happened to him."

Aaron answered them, "Take off the gold earrings that your wives, your sons and your daughters are wearing, and bring them to me." So all the people took off their earrings and brought them to Aaron. He took what they handed him and made it into an idol cast in the shape of a calf, fashioning it with a tool. Then they said, "These are your gods, O Israel, who brought you up out of Egypt."

When Aaron saw this, he built an altar in front of the calf and announced, "Tomorrow there will be a festival to the LORD." So the next day the people rose early and sacrificed burnt offerings and presented fellowship offerings. Afterward they sat down to eat and drink and got up to indulge in revelry.   EXODUS 6:1-6

Boy, that's weird. Build this golden calf and then declare the next day a festival day to Yahweh. You see what's going on here. They're not worshiping the golden calf instead of Yahweh; they're worshiping the golden calf as a representation of Yahweh. Yahweh is out there but he's not showing himself at the moment. What's ironic about this story is that when God does show himself, the people tell him not to ever do that again. They say to Moses, "You tell God to talk to you and then you talk to us, but if he ever does that again we're going to die." But now God is invisible and Moses has disappeared and so they want something that they can see.

I think we're far more likely to be guilty of this kind of idolatry. Somehow we get the nation confused with a visible representative of God. And we think that our deep loyalty and commitment to the nation somehow is service to Yahweh. Soon we think God is especially represented or only represented in our nation. And then we're into the deep water of idolatry. Most of us are guilty of that, by the way.

But what I want to spend most of my time doing is thinking about an even more subtle form of idolatry. How do we know if we are forming people with the gospel or forming them with American culture? Would you deem that to be a fair question? It makes a big difference which one of those you're doing, right? I assume we do not think the purpose of church is to make better American citizens. That's not what we're after. What we're after are totally devoted disciples of Jesus Christ.

So I'm going to offer you a seven-question test. Now the preliminary test to find out whether you are loyal to the gospel or to American culture is how resistant you are to my seven questions. The more resistant you are to my questions, the more obvious it is that you have sold out.

How do we usually evaluate how successful our churches are at forming disciples? We count heads. That is so perversely American. Only Americans would count them. That's not what we're after, right? Would you rather have ten deeply devoted disciples of Jesus Christ or a thousand people just hanging around? Okay, here are my questions. These questions come straight out of my reading of the Bible. We'll find out if we're reading the same Bible. I want you to think about this hypothetical Christian who is a convert. He grew up a real pagan, was converted to Christ, and now has been a Christian for ten years. In that time we would have expected some things to happen, right? Okay, I want to tell you the things that I think would happen if we were forming him into the image of Christ rather than into American culture. And if these things are true for him, they would be true for us.

A SIMPLER LIFE

Number one: "How has my lifestyle been simplified?" A person comes to Jesus Christ as an American, which makes them one of the richest people in the history of the world. They're not head over heels in debt. They've been smarter than that. They've got everything they want. They buy whatever they need. They're doing that ten years after being brought into the community of Jesus Christ. Then we're not doing a very good job of forming, because that's not what disciples do.

It's not the way we think. It's not the way we act. Because we're smarter than that. We know all this stuff is going away anyway. We're not going to invest ourselves in all these things that are going away. We've read Ecclesiastes and we know what will happen. We pile up all this stuff. We get rich and then die. And it's true you can't take it with you. You have to leave it to your idiot of a son. I guess rich people get better coffins, but they all rot. That is the point of Ecclesiastes. They all rot inside.

Having been called into Jesus Christ, one of the first things you would expect to change is the way people view the world of things. Their notions about those should be radically altered. But we live in a culture, we live in a country that is very resistant to that. It pushes us to see our worth in terms of our earnability and our stuff. And the kingdom of God's must stand against that. As we're forming people in the gospel that's one of the things that we expect to happen. So what you need to do is to go into churches and say, "Everybody, we need to evaluate your net wealth and see where it was ten years ago and we've got to get under where it was." So good luck on that.

Friends with the Poor

The second question: "Who are the people from whom I can get nothing and who have come into my home lately?" I have as many friends as most. Usually the reason that they're friends is what they do for me and how they make me feel when I'm around them. I often get a parent telling me how much they appreciate what I've done for their son in my mentoring group. My response is pretty much always the same. "You don't know how your son has blessed me."

But there are those people out there who don't so much bless our lives as wreck them. People Jesus referred to with the wonderful phrase, "the least of these." How do the least of these come into our lives? I was at an academic conference once and heard Gustavo Gutierrez speak. Gustavo is the king of Latin American liberation theology. He's a giant in the theological world. And he's very unusual for a theological giant. He's not really arrogant. He's just kind of there and people are hanging around him. You don't ever hear anybody call him Professor Gutierrez. It's Gustavo. And he's talked for years about being in solidarity with the poor of the world. He was asked, "What does it mean to be in solidarity with the poor?" and he said, "The first thing it means is you have friends who are poor."

That really struck me because most of us don't have friends who are the poorest of the poor. We may have people that we minister to, we may have people we give things to, but very few of us have friends who are the poorest of the poor, people we welcome into our house. But it seems to me that one who has entered into the kingdom of God would start to see those things a bit differently.

CHANGED PRAYING

Question three: "For what and whom do I pray?" I've got this theory that, generally speaking, the prayer lives of Christians and non-Christians are about alike. I think Christians probably lie more about theirs. But I'm thinking they're pretty close to alike. I don't think Christians pray as much as they claim to and I think non-Christians pray more than we think they do. I don't know, is "Oh God" a prayer? It might be. Most of the non-Christians I know have some sort of prayer life.

But I'm not just so much here interested in the frequency of prayer. I'm interested in what are we praying about and who we are praying about. The way we start out in our prayer lives is we pray for ourselves and for those whom we love. We pray for our needs. It's the little boy praying for the new bicycle or the horse. Then we get too sophisticated for that, so we're praying for Great Aunt Maude's cancer. But it all in one way or another comes back to, "God I have some things I need here."

I would expect that as one enters more deeply into the life of the kingdom of God that would change. That we would start to pray in different ways and for different people. My teacher on this is my good friend Bernard of Clairvaux. One of my dead friends. Bernard's got this little essay on the four loves. The first one is the love of self for self's sake. It's totally self-seeking love. Then we finally get past that and we start to love God for self's sake. I love God because of what God does for me. The third one is where we start to love God for God's sake, not because of what he can do for me but just because of who he is. The fourth one is the one that's really interesting, because you don't expect it to be last. He says we learn to love ourselves for God's sake.

That is, we love ourselves in a new way now, not in a selfish way but as instruments of God.

It seems to me he's on to something there, and we would expect our praying to change as we enter more deeply into the kingdom of God. We would start to pray things that aren't directly beneficial to us. We would start to pray more in the spiritual realm and we would start to pray for people who are outside of our world completely. You know there's kind of a prayer renewal going on in our world, but it's not going far enough. Because what we're being encouraged to do is pray more the way we've always prayed. That is, don't just pray for rain, but close the windows thinking you might get some.

What's more important is fundamentally changing who and what we're praying about. Where we don't just pray for ourselves but we open up to pray for the world. Some of you know that I visit a monastery from time to time. Monks pray seven different times during the day. The first one is vigils which is usually around 3:15 a.m. Monks can do this. There's not a lot of night life. And as I pray vigils with the monks, I find something extraordinarily moving in how these monks pray (while the rest of the world sleeps) that God will be standing in protection over the world. I sleep better at night knowing they're doing that. I know they're Catholics, but I still think it counts. I think God honors that.

I find something strangely moving about hearing a monk praying for children who have run away from home and are separated from their parents. It's as if this deep commitment to prayer has not closed them off in the monastery, it's just opened them up to the world. And I would expect as we enter more deeply into the kingdom, our prayer would start to open up into the world. If somebody came and listened to our praying what would they think we cared about?

LOVING SPEECH

Number four: As I enter more deeply into the kingdom this is my question, "How has my speech been affected?" Now James seems to be a bit preoccupied with this. He says the tongue is the last thing to come around, and that's my experience too. Is it yours? I'm not talking about whether the pagan quits cussing or not. I'm expecting that they probably will somewhere along the line (although I'm not totally confident about that). I'm thinking about something deeper than that.

Many of you may have done some Lenten observance leading up to Easter. And I usually do dumb stuff. I drink way too much soda pop, Coke, Dr. Pepper, you know, the whole nine yards. What I usually give up for Lent is my Coke addiction (no, not that kind of coke). I decided this year to do something bolder than that, so I decided to do two things for Lent. One was the Jesus prayer, "Lord Jesus Christ, have mercy on me a sinner." There are a few different versions of it, but that's the heart of it. You kind of do it as you breathe and it becomes part of your rhythm. I decided to do 300 of those a day. I get an A+ on that one.

The second thing I decided to do I get a C- on. You know I talk way too much. It's not just that I keep too hectic a speaking schedule, that's obvious. It's that I talk too much. And a lot of well meaning people out there contribute to my addiction to speech. They keep asking me stuff. Somebody will ask me about something I really don't know anything about. Then I will proceed to talk about it. You see how addicted I am.

So I decided to make this commitment. I couldn't take a vow of silence because I had teaching and preaching responsibilities; that was just impractical. So I decided to do another kind of monastic discipline. I decided to hold myself to this: I would speak only what love required and if love didn't require it, I wouldn't say it.

I'm wandering around the ACU campus and someone asks, "Do you know where such and such a building is?" The loving thing to do is to say, "Yes I do, there it is," and so that's what I would say. And when a student comes to my office and says, "I'm really struggling with this concept you covered in class, could you explain it to me?" I would say, "Sure, I would be happy to do that. Let me explain it to you," because that would be the loving thing to do. But I would not say any words that were not required by love.

I got off to a great start the first hour. After that it got a little rocky. A few in my mentoring group decided to enter into this with me. They didn't do a whole lot better than I did, so that made me feel better. It was just a wonderful learning experience. I've now decided to accept this discipline for a little while longer. What was striking to me is how little of my speech came from the deep well of love. Instead, much of my speech was mean, trivial, and caustic. And that's not even getting into pride.

How much of your speech is driven by the desire to show what you know or who you are? Well, here's my theory. Most of us in churches don't talk a whole lot different than anybody else does. Oh, we may curse less. But what drives our speech doesn't seem to be very different from what drives theirs. As we enter more deeply into discipleship with Jesus Christ that should change. And that's very counter to American culture, because in American culture speech is one of the weapons we use. Speech is one of the things you use to win. You try to whip people. You try to out-speechify them.

Changed Desires

Number five: "How are you doing with your desires?" How have your desires changed over these last ten years since you've become a Christian? Do you need your television less? Most people (if not addicted) are in a deep relationship with their television. Has my relationship with the internet changed? Has my relationship with drugs or alcohol, sex in some cases, has that changed? Has my relationship with golf changed? Has my relationship with sports changed? How am I doing with the stuff that really had a grip on me before I came to Jesus Christ?

I've got a theory. You can't tell a lot of difference about those things between Christians and other Americans. Because one of the things we try to do in America is give you as many addictions as possible because they pay the bills. We have a whole industry in America whose one task is to get you to desire things you don't really need. And they spend a lot of time thinking about how to do it. And they're good at it. All you have to do is look through my house. Look at that thing. I cannot believe I bought you. You are not what you were cracked up to be.

Reconciling Relationships

Number six: "What's happened to my relationships?" We live in a society that throws away everything including relationships. Are our relationships more enduring? Are they more solid? Are they more committed by virtue of our engagement in the community of faith? Are our relationships the ones that generate peace and the dissolving of lines or do they create line-drawing and conflict? I wonder how we could have walked with Jesus as long as we have and not gotten any better at relationships than we are. You know, I'll be with somebody and I later think, "Boy, I treated them badly."

And in church sometimes we'll treat each other in ways that nobody in the world would ever think about treating us. How in the world can we have been in the community of faith all this time and think that we could treat each other that way? Are churches the places where lines dissolve and all people are one? It would be a little hard to make that case and I'm not just talking about denominational lines now, although that's bad enough.

It's well documented that the most segregated moment in American life is at 10:00 A.M. on Sunday. Every aspect of American society is more deeply integrated than churches. How does that happen? We're deeply into a relationship with Jesus Christ that hasn't fundamentally changed our relationships. Do I see my relationships in a redemptive way? I'm not talking about a manipulative way. I'm talking about entering into relationships hoping that people will experience the reconciling work of God in Christ. Because that's who we are. That's what we do. I don't know. I'm not convinced reconciliation is our best thing.

Indifference to Circumstances

Number seven: "Have I become increasingly indifferent to circumstances?" Because as we enter into the world of Jesus Christ the circumstances in which we find ourselves matter less and less. You know Paul is my hero in this. He says, "I've known what it is to have a lot of stuff and I've known what it is to have nothing," and then he says, "I can do all things through Christ who gives me strength." That's in the context of contentment. When I'm healthy

I'm good, and when I'm sick I'm good, because I'm relatively indifferent to those circumstances. Because for me to live is Christ and to die is gain.

I tell my students Paul is my hero because he is impossible to corrupt. Now I think he was difficult. I don't know him personally but I think he was difficult. If you look through the text he has a little trouble getting along with almost everybody. But boy, he's hard to corrupt. You can't buy him off. You take everything from him and he says, "I count all things lost for Jesus Christ. I don't have anything, what are you going to take?" You threaten to kill him. He says, "For me to die is gain." So you let him live. "For me to live is Christ." That is one tough Christian right there. Virtually incorruptible.

Now we live in a culture that tells us circumstances are everything. It's about how healthy you are and it's about how wealthy you are and it's about how comfortable you are and it's about where you live. Location, location, location. It's all about trying to get control of your circumstances. We want to make sure we can control the situation. None of us like to be out of control. Every once in a while it's really good to throw yourself into a situation where you can't control the circumstances. One of the ways I do this is I have a favorite Tex-Mex restaurant that I like to go to and take others to. I always tell them, "Okay, here are the rules of this restaurant. You can order whatever you want, but you have to take whatever they bring. These often have very little to do with each other. Just get used to being a little out of control here."

Most of you have been in circumstances when you were in another country where you were totally helpless. I can remember the first time I went to Nigeria, which coincidentally was the last time I went to Nigeria. I was totally unprepared. They didn't tell me much because they did not think I would go if they did. So I arrived in the Lagos airport, chaos all around me, and I am helpless. I don't know what's going on. It's hot. My bag doesn't come. It finally comes and I'm trying to get through customs and they've opened my bag and they're going through it painstakingly. The chief customs agent and I have a conversation I do not understand. It was in English but I did not understand it. Oh, I understood the words but I did not understand it.

"It's very hot in here."

"Yes, it is."

"These men are working very hard."

"Yes, they are and I appreciate it."

The guy was rolling his eyes. "Do you have something for these men?"

I finally said, "Yes, yes, yes. I do, I do, I do." I give them a couple of dollars and I'm on my way.

I'm in this strange country and I'm helpless. I mean I am helpless. I talked to the missionaries later about this experience and they that I should not pay bribes. I was there a couple of weeks. So on my way out of the country, I remembered what they said. At the airport I'm clicking through things and I've gotten through and I'm almost to the promised land. One more person stops me and says, "Let me look in your bag." He starts looking in my carry-on bag. And he pulls out my pill bottle. I'm quite claustrophobic and I have a lot of trouble flying, so when I fly long distances I basically fly sedated.

So he pulls my pills out and says, "These are very strong pills."

"Yes they are. Put them back."

"This is a hallucinogen."

"It is not. It is a tranquilizer. Put it back."

"This is an illegal drug."

"It is not. It is a prescription drug. Put it back."

"You can not have this drug in this country."

"So deport me."

So we had a little longer conversation and I am getting more and more nervous and thinking about what my future life might look like in jail in Nigeria.

I could not control these circumstances and this was just a reminder all over again of how much I wanted to. Because I've been taught that you can control your circumstances and you must control your circumstances because your circumstances are the key to your happiness. So you take care of your health and try to get enough money to be comfortable and you live in the right neighborhood and send your kids to the right schools and eat at the right places and you have the right friends—because our circumstances are the key to our happiness. But as we enter more deeply into discipleship with Jesus Christ our circumstances become increasingly indifferent to us. And if they don't, we're not doing it right.

Now the question we have today is, "Would I be okay in some place other than America? Am I okay with something other than the American way of life or is my well being and happiness somehow tied to the circumstances that the American system has produced?" If it is, we need to get over that. That is a pretty ugly form of nationalism.

I am a loyal citizen. At some fairly deep level I love family. I love country. I love friends. I love the church with which I currently worship. But if all those circumstances should change, I hope I would still know how to love God. God's mission does not depend on the export of the American way of life. If I'm right about anything today, the export of the American way of life is more likely to lead us away from the kingdom of God than toward it, because it is seductive in these seven ways that I have described. We need to become increasingly indifferent to that way of life. It doesn't mean you don't obey the law. It doesn't mean you don't love the country. It just means you have less and less invested in all of those circumstances. Because that's not where God's eternal kingdom is.

You don't have to think what I think. You don't have to do what I do. What I would really like you to do is start to think about this stuff. Because Christians are often perceived as those who are primarily holding up a certain form of American culture as much as they are the gospel of Jesus Christ. And if you don't think that people think that, you need to go out and talk to some pagans and see what they think of the face of American Christianity. But if they meet some live Christians they'll find out that we're not necessarily who they think we are. But we've got to create some deeply devoted disciples of Jesus Christ for whom the tune is being called by Jesus Christ and not the culture in which we live. That will change the way we think and talk and act and react to the world in which we belong. And I think we are far down the line toward becoming a deeply acculturated people. I won't say we've sold our soul to the American dream. I'll just say we're on the market.

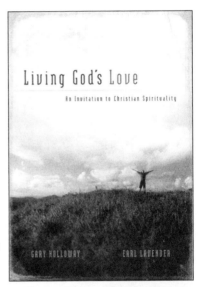

The Meditative Commentary Series

An exciting new Bible study tool for your group.

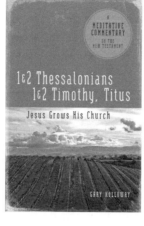

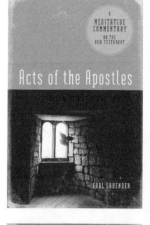

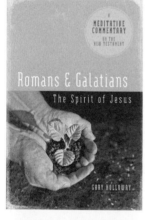

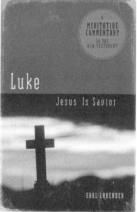

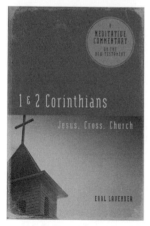

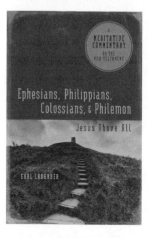

Matthew
Jesus Is King
by Gary Holloway
$13.99   ISBN 0-9767790-1-3

Thessalonians, Timothy, & Titus
Jesus Grows His Church
by Gary Holloway
$11.99   ISBN 0-89112-503-5

Acts of the Apostles
Jesus Alive in His Church
by Earl Lavender
$13.99   ISBN 0-89112-501-9

Romans & Galatians
The Spirit of Jesus
by Gary Holloway
$11.99   ISBN 0-89112-502-7

Luke
Jesus Is Savior
by Earl Lavender
$13.99   ISBN 0-89112-500-0

1 & 2 Corinthians
Jesus, Cross, Church
by Earl Lavender
$11.99   ISBN 978-0-89112-568-6

Ephesians, Philippians,
Colossians, & Philemon
Jesus Above All
by Earl Lavender
$9.99   ISBN 978-0-89112-561-7

TWELVE VOLUMES COVERING THE NEW TESTAMENT

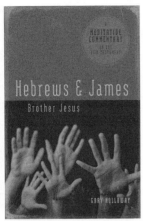

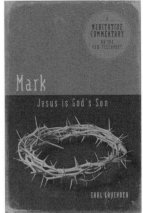

Hebrews & James
Brother Jesus
by Gary Holloway
$10.99   ISBN 978-0-89112-505-1

John
Believing in Jesus
by Gary Holloway
$10.99   ISBN 978-0-89112-504-4

Mark
Jesus is God's Son
by Earl Lavender
$11.99 ISBN 978-0-89112-551-8

Revelation
Jesus the Conquering
by Terry Briley
$10.99   ISBN 978-0-89112-559-4

Peter, John, & Jude
Living in Jesus
by Gary Holloway
$8.99   ISBN 978-0-89112-557-0

*Hear the authors introduce the series
and tell how to use it. Call for a free CD.*

QUANTITY DISCOUNTS AVAILABLE

LEAFWOOD
P U B L I S H E R S

To order call toll free 1-877-816-4455
Or ask for these books at your favorite bookstore